NomosTextbook

The textbook series presents selected topics from the social sciences and humanities program. Published are outstanding topics relevant to English-language teaching from all program areas, such as political science, sociology, social work, or media and communication studies. The selection of books is based on the curricula of the respective disciplines. Renowned experts provide a compact introduction to the topics of the respective subject.

Peter G. Kirchschlaeger

Ethical Decision-Making

Nomos

This English edition is based on the book "Ethisches Entscheiden", Nomos 2023, ISBN 978-3-7560-1317-3. Parts of the translation into English were created with support of machine translation and/or artificial intelligence.

The Deutsche Nationalbibliothek lists this publication in the Deutsche Nationalbibliografie; detailed bibliographic data are available on the Internet at http://dnb.d-nb.de

ISBN 978-3-7560-1341-8 (Print)
978-3-7489-1868-4 (ePDF)

British Library Cataloguing-in-Publication Data
A catalogue record for this book is available from the British Library.

ISBN 978-3-7560-1341-8 (Print)
978-3-7489-1868-4 (ePDF)

Library of Congress Cataloging-in-Publication Data
Kirchschlaeger, Peter G.
Ethical Decision-Making
Peter G. Kirchschlaeger
140 pp.
Includes bibliographic references and index.

ISBN 978-3-7560-0637-3 (Print)
978-3-7489-4267-2 (ePDF)

Online Version
Nomos eLibrary

1st Edition 2023

For our daughter Sara Alexandra

Foreword

Thanks to our freedom, ethical decision-making challenges us as human beings on a daily basis – be it in our private or professional lives, be it on an individual, organizational or institutional level, be it in a social, economic or political context. The opportunities open to us thanks to successful ethical decision-making and the challenges to be mastered in this regard are increasing – because of growing ethical complexity and because of a reality that is increasingly presenting itself as a VUCA world (VUCA stands for volatility, uncertainty, complexity, and ambiguity) (Hieronymi, 2016, pp. 6-21).

In view of these realities and thanks to the exchange with students, with participants in conferences, meetings, research workshops, events in which I had the opportunity to participate or lead, with politically engaged people, with decision-makers in politics, society and business, as well as with colleagues and scholars from other scientific disciplines, the idea of developing a model that strives to address new opportunities and challenges that arise in the course of ethical decision-making and that strives to address new opportunities and challenges that arise in the course of ethical decision-making and to encourage a well-founded ethical position and corresponding action, and that in these respects goes beyond existing models and instruments of ethical decision-making has matured in me – this, of course, in the awareness that I may not do justice to all existing instruments and models of ethical decision-making. At the same time, my goal was to develop a model that supports ethical decision-making with ease and argumentative elegance. And out came: SAMBA!

SAMBA stands for the following four steps:

1. See and Understand the Reality
2. Analyze the Reality from a Moral Standpoint
3. Be the Ethical Judge!
4. Act Accordingly!

More about this now follows in this book.

A book goes back to an intellectual path that one never treads entirely alone, but on which one directly or indirectly as well as implicitly and explicitly, picks up, collects or receives suggestions and impulses. My special thanks go to the team members of the Institute for Social Ethics ISE of the Faculty of Theology of the University of Lucerne – Aaron Butler, Adrienne Hochuli Stillhard, Alexandra Kaiser-Duliba, Andrea Murer, Antonia Bilic, Dr. Ana Laura Edelhoff, Dr. Ernst von Kimakowitz, Dr. Evelyne Tauchnitz, Dr. Juerg Kuehnis, Kiki Kuenzler, Matteo Frey, Melina Faeh, Shania Kuhn, Sonia Arfaoui –, the participants of the Lucerne Graduate School in Ethics LGSE of the Institute of Social Ethics ISE of the Faculty of Theology of the University of Lucerne – a.o. Elizaveta Ebner, Noemi Honegger, Sara Ilić, Mojalefa Koloko, Laurence Lerch, Darius Meier, Jan Thomas Otte, Nina Stern, Stefanie Uhl and Matej Vereš –, the faculty and students of the Lucerne Summer University: Ethics in a Global Context under the patronage of UNESCO of the Institute of Social Ethics ISE of the Faculty of Theology of the University of Lucerne, my students at the University of Lucerne and at other universities in Switzerland and abroad, the participants of conferences, meetings and events in which I had the opportunity to participate or lead. At the same time, I would like to thank the other members, including of the Mobility 4.0 working group of the Swiss Federal Roads Office (FEDRO), the Swiss Federal Ethics Committee on Non-Human Biotechnology ECNH, and the board of trustees of the Swiss Foundation of the European Academy of Sciences and Arts, from whom I learn or had the opportunity to learn a lot.

The research-oriented academic environment at the Faculty of Theology of the University of Lucerne has greatly facilitated the writing of this book, for which I am very grateful.

I would especially like to thank Mr. Alexander Hutzel of Nomos Verlag for including the study in the series "NomosTextbook". In setting up the manuscript for printing, Ms. Eva Lang from Nomos Verlag as well as Ms. Antonia Bilic, Ms. Kiki Kuenzler, and Ms. Shania Kuhn from the ISE were of great help to me, for which I am very grateful.

My wife Miriam and our daughters Sara and Mia, my entire family and my friends have accompanied the development of this book with their love and friendship, with encouraging interest and with great support. All my thanks go to the people of my "little world".

Lucerne, July 13, 2023 Peter G. Kirchschlaeger

Table of Contents

1 Why Ethics-SAMBA? 11

1.1 Need for Ethical Decisions 11
1.2 Expectations of Ethical Decision-Making 17

2 Ethics in a Global Context 25

3 Ethics and Law 33

4 Human Ethical Decisions Are and Will Remain in Demand – Also in the Future 39

4.1 Delegating Ethical Decisions to Machines? 39
4.2 Vulnerability 40
4.3 Conscience 44
4.4 Freedom 48
4.5 Responsibility 49
4.6 Autonomy 50
4.7 Ethical Decisions of Humans 53

5 The Rule-Transcending Uniqueness of the Concrete 57

5.1 Ethics Is not Democracy 57
5.2 Ethics Beyond Principles and Norms 57

6 SAMBA 59

6.1 See and Understand the Reality 60
6.2 Analyze the Reality from a Moral Standpoint 62
Virtue Ethics 65
Normethics 66
Authoritative Approaches 66
Natural Law 66
Discourse Ethics 66
Teleology / Consequentialism 67
Utilitarianism 67
Deontology (Duty Ethics) 69
The Principle of Responsibility 70
The Principle of Justice 79
Human Rights Principles 89
6.3 Be the Ethical Judge! 109
Excursus: Ethics Committees, Ethics Boards, Ethics Commissions, Ethics Councils, Ethics Teams, Ethics Groups in the Hands of Ethicists! 117
6.4 Act Accordingly! 119

7 Outlook: Ethics-SAMBA. With Ease and Argumentative Elegance To Take Ethical Decisions in 4 Steps 123

Bibliography 125

Index 139

1 Why Ethics-SAMBA?

Summary

In this chapter, you will learn that thanks to our freedom and self-determination, we humans have to make ethical decisions all the time. Ethical decision-making is based neither on legal considerations nor on self-interest, individual interest, or economic rationality, nor on pragmatic or practical considerations, but is oriented toward the good and seeks the right. Ethics as a science that reflects on morality should help here and provide orientation. At the same time, its practical orientation is expressed in the fact that ethical decisions should also lead to corresponding ethical actions.

In the course of its striving for universality, ethics must respect the principle of generalizability through rational and plausible arguments to safeguard both freedom and human dignity – the two principles that constitute ethics – of every human being, as well as a cultural, religious, ideological, moral, and ethical plurality. "Good reasons" are to be identified. A model of how "good reasons" can be identified, or how criteria can be formulated that distinguish "good reasons" from other reasons, is as follows: "Good reasons" means that it must be conceivable that all people, in their effective freedom and autonomy as well as in their full equality would agree to these reasons – within a model of thought and not within a real worldwide referendum – on ethical grounds (see Kirchschlaeger, 2021a).

People can help with their ideas and actions today and tomorrow to help shape the today and the tomorrow. For this to happen on an ethical basis and for individuals and society to assume more ethical responsibility, four competencies are needed: first, it is important to perceive reality as comprehensively as possible. Second, we need the ability to recognize ethical opportunities and risks as such. This requires ethical reflection competency. This also includes the rationally justifiable choice of (an) ethical reference point(s), with the help of which the ethical opportunities and risks can be identified. Third, it is necessary to take an ethically justified position. Fourth, ethically based proposals for solutions and possible courses of action are helpful.

Ethics-SAMBA as a model for ethical decision-making can help here.

1.1 Need for Ethical Decisions

The changes in our living environment open up scope for action for us humans and at the same time present us with new challenges of relevance to society as a whole.[1] The need for ethical orientation in an increasingly complex world is growing. This gives rise to numerous fundamental questions with new urgency, such as: How do we confront global problems such as poverty, pandemics, or climate change? How do we deal responsibly with expanded possibilities for action in medicine and biotechnology? What does digital transformation mean for the future of our work, for economic and political systems, for us as individuals and as a society, and for our lives? How can we reconcile the legitimate freedom

1 All verbatim quotations originally written in languages other than English have been translated with support of machine translation and/or artificial intelligence.

of individuals and those of society? What significance does the perception of personal, social, political, and global responsibility have in this context? "The question of what is right and good arises for every society, every generation, and every person" (Pauder-Studer, 2020, p. 13).

Ethical decisions are required – whether at an individual level (micro level), at the level of organizations (meso level), or the level of societies, institutions, or the global society (macro level). They also serve to understand our understanding, i.e. they allow us to identify where opportunities and risks exist from an ethical perspective, as well as where and how opportunities are to be benefitted from and risks to be mastered. The focus of ethical decision-making is neither on legal considerations nor on self-interest, individual interest, or economic rationality, nor on pragmatic, or practical considerations. "Ethics means philosophical reflection on what is right or wrong on moral grounds. [...] The term 'ethics' is most often used synonymously with 'morality', i.e. synonymous with the sum of the norms by which we consider it right and well-founded to live." (Pauder-Studer, 2020, p. 14). The focus is thus on what people should or should not do. These questions of 'ought' only arise when people are thought in conjunction with freedom. Thanks to freedom people are free to decide between "good" and "bad" or between "right" and "wrong". If people did not have freedom in such a fundamental sense, then the question of *ethical* decisions would be superfluous and this book would end here or would never have begun.

The freedom of human beings also includes the autonomy of human beings. "Only when a person no longer allows him- or herself to be dogmatically dictated what is good, but determines it for him- or herself after careful consideration, i.e., at a critical distance from his or her own interests as well as from the judgments of others, what goals are good for him or her, for a group of people, or all people as a whole, has he or she achieved the moral dimension" (Pieper, 2017, p. 19). This autonomy allows people to relate to morality, to expose points of orientation for ethical decision-making, and to make ethical decisions. "Morality or morals are those patterns of action which have emerged from processes of mutual recognition in a community of people and which have been distinguished as generally binding and to which normative validity is attributed. The terms morality and custom thus denote structures of order that represent evolved forms of life, forms of life that reflect the value and meaning concepts of a community of action" (Ibid., p. 22).

At this point, however, a significant distinction would have to be made, which would clearly show what is important in *ethics* and thus in *ethical decisions.* "Whoever does not leave it at simply judging morally, but is interested in what is actually moral and whether it makes any sense at all to act morally, how one can justify such action – whoever asks such questions begins to pursue ethics. Ethics discusses all problems connected with morality on a more general, fundamental, and insofar more abstract level by reconstructing in a purely *formal way* the conditions that must be fulfilled in order for an action, no matter what its content in detail, can rightly be called a *moral* act. Ethics thus does not determine which concrete individual goals are morally good goals worth striving for by everyone;

rather, it determines the criteria according to which it can be bindingly established in the first place what goal is to be recognized as a good goal. Ethics does not say what the good is in concreto, but how one comes to judge something as good. [...] Ethics is not itself a morality but talks *about* morality" (Pieper, 2017, p. 20, emphasis in original). Ethics is therefore not morality but thinks about morality. Ethics is the science that thinks about morality and reflects and examines it. The following examples serve to illustrate this point: "Analogous to the literary scholar and theater critic, the ethicist also judges this object, namely morality, from a certain distance to his object. By doing ethics, the ethicist does not act morally, but reflects on morality from a theoretical perspective and thus from the critical distance of the scientist" (Pieper, 2017, p. 25).

This does not mean, of course, that ethics and thus ethical decisions have nothing to do with practice. On the contrary, ethics as a science is characterized by its practical orientation. Nevertheless, ethics and ethical decisions have to be differentiated from concrete moral or ethical actions, which is illustrated by the following analogy: "The object of literary science is the so-called 'beautiful literature', which is examined and classified under various aspects (e.g. linguistic, formal-technical, content-related). Those who pursue literary studies do not write a novel, a poem, etc by doing so, although they may well be capable of it; rather, they analyze literary texts with regard to certain regular structural elements and forms in order to arrive at general statements about 'the' novel, 'the' drama, 'the' ode, etc., and, by means of these rules, they in turn attempt to critically assess individual novels, dramas, odes. Whoever writes a novel, on the other hand, does not engage in 'literary studies,' although knowledge of literary studies can certainly be of use to him in the writing process" (Pieper, 2017, p. 24f). Ethics informs ethical and moral action.

The first step of an ethical action turns out to be ethical decision-making. At the same time, ethics and ethical decision-making have to keep a sufficient distance from the practice. Only in this way can a critical penetration of practice by ethics succeed.

The concept of ethics as a science that thinks about morality and thus has its object of investigation in morality, seems to have become clearer than it seems to be the case with the concept of morality. "The concept of morality encompasses all structures of order and meaning (systems of rules), some of which have arisen naturally, some of which have been agreed upon by convention, some of which have been handed down by tradition, and which have emerged from processes of mutual recognition and values regulate the satisfaction of the needs of a human community of action on the one hand and, on the other hand, provide information on what is generally regarded as binding (as a duty). Duties provide information about the community's understanding of freedom." (Pieper, 2017, p. 37) Morality can be located on the personal level (individual) and the social level (community, society).

Ethical decision-making is nourished by morality which, however, has to be reflected ethically. Ethical decisions get their meaning from ethically reflected morality. "In the concept of morality, freedom is thought as the unconditional claim, to realize freedom for the sake of freedom as the highest human good. [...] Morality (in the sense of ἦθος) is the will to do good that has made the unconditional claim of freedom its own and its horizon of meaning. Whoever acts out of this basic attitude possesses *moral competence.*" (Pieper, 2017, p. 37f, emphasis in original)

In the interplay of morality and morals, ethics has an essential task, which also has a constitutive effect on ethical decision-making. "This *interrelationship of morality and morals,* which founds human practice as a humane practice, is the central subject of ethics: Ethics reflects the relationship between morality and morals. By setting in motion the dialectic of morality and morals, ethics fulfills its critical purpose, namely, by going back and forth between the conditional claims of morality on the one hand, and the unconditional claim of the principle of morality on the other, to set in motion a process of enlightenment through which dogmatic fixations, prejudices, and constraints on action are made transparent or dissolved" (Pieper, 2017, p. 39, emphasis in original). This exclusive focus on the unconditioned is what distinguishes ethics. It is concerned with "the good in itself" or "the right in itself". "The morally good is what, on a final level of evaluation, becomes recognizable to us not as any good, but as good par excellence, and at the same time obligates us unconditionally" (Marschuetz, 2014, p. 20).

This can be further illustrated if we contrast judgments where, for example, "good" is used in the course of an everyday value judgment (e.g., "good food"), a certain quality is designated in relation to a sensuary perception. In an instrumental understanding, the statement "good for something" (as a means to an end) comes into play. Pragmatically, something is "good for someone" (goal). Distinct from all three uses is the moral use of "good,“ which understands "good" as "good in itself" (in the sense of unconditional validity). "Ethics, insofar as it wishes to provide a sufficient justification of morality, must refer to an unconditional, ultimate validity that guarantees its normative claim. Ethics understands this unconditional in the principle of morality as freedom and indeed as freedom which has no reason outside of itself, but is self-grounded. Wherever human action appears with a claim to morality, it is claimed to have acted or to want to act unconditionally good. Unconditionally good, however, can only mean an action which is *both done out of* freedom *as well as with* freedom (of the agent and of those affected by the act) as its goal." (Pieper, 2017, p. 41, emphasis in original)

How does this concentration of ethics on the unconditional aspect work, if, at the same time, it considers morality in its changeability and dynamics? Doesn't it make it a target for the accusation of relativism (i.e. that actually everything can be ethically acceptable and everything ethically problematic in the sense of "anything goes")? "This objection applies only to the variable substantive moment in morality (e.g. to live according to the principle of polygamy [...]), but overlooks the fact that an invariable formal moment is also expressed in genuine moral claims to validity (e.g. to live according to the principle to live and to act always and everywhere unconditionally good), which does not merge in any special morality, but as a principle of morality underlies any concretion of freedom. [...] The fact, however, that from one and the same basic norm (e.g. the norm of human dignity) in different cultural circles different, sometimes even contradictory rules are derived as general instructions for action, is not an objection against the validity of the norm, but challenges us to search for ever more perfect forms of a common order of life, for an ever better, more humane morality to search for" (Pieper, 2017, p. 42). In this regard, it is up to ethics to provide clarity concerning the interaction of morality and morals. This determination of the relationship between morality and morals affects ethical decisions since, thanks to morality, they know their clear orientation towards the unconditional and, with a critical distance of ethics, the conditional of morals.

Ethical decision-making is and will remain necessary because ethics does not take ethical decisions by telling humans exactly what they have to do, but out of respect for and consideration of the freedom of all people – like a compass. "The compass does [...] not directly prescribe the right path, but indicates how the right path is to be determined. If one transfers this image of the compass to ethics, it becomes clear that its function does not consist in directly enjoining a certain action; it always only enjoins morality as the freedom essential to human beings. Nevertheless, it provides information on how to determine the morally appropriate action in an individual case, provided that the agent knows sufficiently about the situation in which he finds himself and has, from this existing situation, an idea of the future situation to be striven for, which is to be realized by his action. Just as the compass indicates the direction to the north as a fixed, immovable point of reference that makes it possible to determine the way to a desired place, so ethics points to the idea of freedom as that unconditional point of reference from which an action can be determined as intended from the relationship between its point of departure and destination. But just as the compass only helps its user to find the right way, without being able to force him to actually go the way that has been recognized as the right one, so ethics only guides the agent to determine his will morally without being able to force him to actually perform the action recognized as moral" (Pieper, 2017, p. 98).

Ethics as a science that reflects on the good and right living, contributes to the clarification of moral conflicts, examines the legitimacy of the claims to the validity of moral positions and provides orientation in moral questions and ethical decision-making processes. Ethical decision-making is in demand – yesterday, today, tomorrow, and the day after tomorrow. The human fascination with the questions of what man wants to be, what kind of world he dreams of, and whether everything that man can technically do should also be done, turns out not to be an achievement of the 21st century. It dates back far into the history of mankind and will not disappear in the foreseeable future. With their ideas, decisions, and actions, people can help shape today and tomorrow.

But how can current and future ethical opportunities and risks be identified? Numerous issues of public discussion have an ethical dimension at their core. Ethical issues also play an increasingly important role in everyday professional life. Not only in healthcare and research but also in companies, private and public institutions, as well as in the decision-making and actions of individuals. Accordingly, the need for ethical decisions has grown in recent years. To meet this need, as well as the wish to assume more ethical responsibility as individuals and society, four competencies are necessary:

- *First,* reality must be perceived as comprehensively as possible.
- *Second,* it requires the ability to recognize ethical opportunities and risks as such. This requires ethical reflection competency. This also includes the rationally justifiable choice of (an) ethical reference point(s) which helps in identifying the ethical opportunities and risks.
- *Third,* it is important to take an ethically justified position.
- *Fourth,* ethically based proposals for solutions and possible actions are helpful.

Furthermore, ethical reflection is also characterized by the fact that it tries to answer to the questions of what for, where to, and why in a justifiably reliable and generally binding manner. Ethics is a science that reflects on morality. As a scientific discipline, ethics seeks knowledge of what ought to be in a rational, logically coherent, methodically reflexive and systematic way. Ethics strives for a universally justifiable notion of right and wrong, good and bad, even across generations. Universality as a necessary characteristic of ethics, ethical assertions, ethical principles, and ethical norms requires the fulfillment of the principle of generalizability through rational and plausible arguments. "Good reasons" are to be presented. A model of how to identify "good reasons" or formulate criteria that distinguish "good reasons" from other reasons is as follows: *"Good reasons" means that it must be conceivable that all people, in their effective freedom and autonomy as well as in their full equality would agree to these reasons – within a model of thought and not within a real worldwide referendum – on ethical grounds.* (see Kirchschlaeger, 2021a)

The need for rational justification is an expression of the respect for freedom and human dignity of each individual, for the plurality of secular society, and for ethics itself. Underlying this, I would suggest, is a concept of secularity that goes beyond understanding secularity as "a state of increasing pluralization of religious and non-religious possibilities" (Casanova, 2015, p. 19) or goes even further, in that it is concerned with *the reality of guaranteeing, protecting, and promoting a growing plurality of religious and nonreligious options.*

Finally, what is ethically required should not change from one day to the next, even under the conditions of a changing reality. It achieves this by aligning the ethically required with the core of the reason-based unconditional, which is made up of the *two principles of all principles of ethics freedom and human dignity*:

- The ethical principle of freedom – i.e. to think all people with freedom – initiates ethics and the related necessity of ethical decision-making (in the freedom to choose between ethically right and wrong – ethically good and bad) and establishes the moral capability of human beings.

Freedom means acting according to one's own wishes and plans. It can include the freedom to want what one wants and the freedom to want what one does not want. The latter means that freedom can also mean wanting what is "wanted", i.e., what is ethically wanted, even though this may not correspond to one's desires, needs, preferences, lusts, or interests. This opens up the social horizon of freedom because the freedom of all other people as well as the human dignity of all human beings and the corresponding responsibilities come into focus.

- The ethical principle of human dignity of all human beings establishes the uniqueness of *all* human beings, distinguishes them from material objects and other forms of life, completely forbids putting a price tag on human beings and instrumentalizing them, and gives ethics a basis and a framework at the same time. What is at stake in the ethical principle of human dignity is aptly expressed in the phrase "everybody matters" (Appiah, 2006, p. 144).

Neither the freedom nor the human dignity of all people loses any of their validity in the face of the latest scientific findings or the latest technological developments.

1.2 Expectations of Ethical Decision-Making

Can't the need for ethical decisions as just explained not be covered by existing models and instruments? Why is there a need for a new model of ethical decision-making when there is already an abundance of models and instruments for ethical decision-making? Existing approaches to ethical decision-making allow to discover and identify points and aspects that perhaps deserve more attention and thus should be covered in the Ethics-SAMBA. On the other hand, thanks to the models and instruments of ethical decision-making already in circulation, it is possible to identify core elements in which primary expectations of ethical decision-making manifest themselves. (This reference to already existing models and instruments of ethical decision-making is made with epistemic modesty. Of course, no claim can be made to a globally comprehensive and conclusive overview, nor is one immune from not doing justice to certain models and instruments due to the brevity of the respective explanations. The intention to identify essential points and aspects and, in this sense, to systematize and reduce these approaches to be able to critically evaluate them for this project, is an additional complication in this respect).

In both respects, Ethics-SAMBA can learn from already existing models and instruments. A critical examination of existing approaches reveals that this wealth and diversity of projects can help to answer the question of how ethical decision-making can succeed. First, they basically aim to strengthen the ethical legitimacy of decision-making which, despite possible weaknesses or gaps in a model or instrument in a particular context or situation can be successful. Second, regardless of their persuasiveness, they each expose specific aspects of ethical decision-making.

The models and instruments of ethical decision-making available to date lack the action orientation of ethics as a science, which should also be reflected in a model of ethical decision-making. This becomes clear, for example, in the following model: "A partir del análisis de los modelos que se han descrito para abordar los dilemas éticos, se pudieron identificar cuatro etapas en el proceso de revisión. Las etapas son las siguientes: 1) identificar el dilema ético; 2) hacer explícitos los hechos relevantes para la discusión del dilema; 3) exponer las posturas éticas; y 4) tomar una decisión"[2] (Ruiz-Cano, 2015, p. 97). This desideratum is to be addressed in a new model for ethical decision-making.

Furthermore, a new model aims to more accurately account for rapidly advancing technical progress and its potential impact on human ethical decision-making.

In addition, SAMBA is also intended to more specifically address the complexity of ethics – taking into account and considering *the rule-transcending uniqueness of the concrete* in its consequences for ethical decision making.

Moreover, it can always be tried to be even more compact and concise in ethical decision-making while maintaining argumentative elegance and ease.

Beyond that, existing models and instruments show significant and further-reaching aspects for the development of a new approach. For example, the **Integrative Descriptive Model of Ethical Decision Making by K. C. Strong and D. G. Meyer** (see Strong & Meyer, 1992), where the focus lies on the managers' decision-making. In this model, the ethical responsibility and the ethical decision-making as embedded in managerial decision-making is considered. Ethical decisions are assigned a specific place, which leads to the question – which also has to be answered in Ethics-SAMBA – where ethical decision-making should be located, for example in its relation to law.

2 From the analysis of the models that have been described for dealing with ethical dilemmas, four stages in the review process could be identified. The stages are as follows: 1) identify the ethical dilemma; 2) make explicit the facts relevant to the discussion of the dilemma; 3) state the ethical positions; and 4) make a decision.

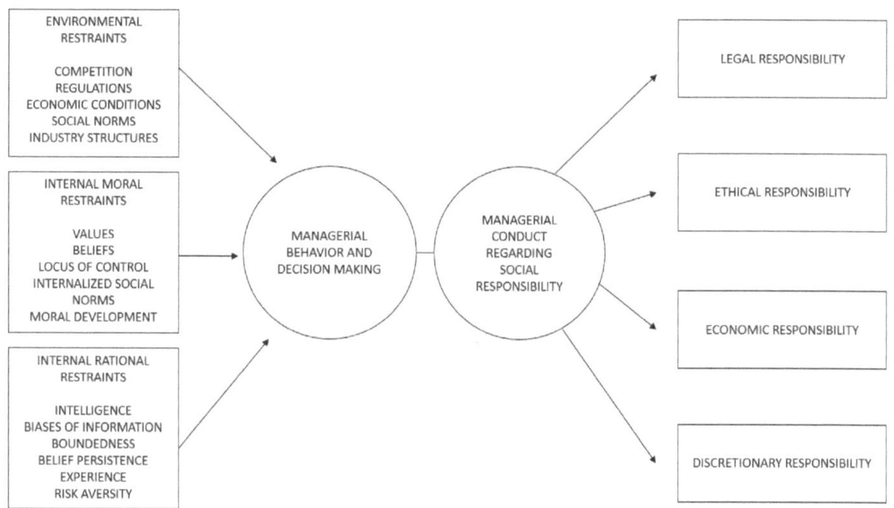

Figure 1: Integrative Descriptive Model of Ethical Decision Making. Source: Strong & Meyer, 1992, p. 97.

Finally, a consensus can also be identified for the expected content areas that a model for ethical decision-making should cover, as illustrated by the following five models:

"EDM process endorsed by ACA" (Forester-Miller & David, 1995).

1. "Identify the Problem
   Tune Into Feelings
   Involve Clients in Process
2. Consider Moral Principles
3. Review Relevant Codes, Laws, and Regulations
4. Consult
5. Identify Desired Outcomes
6. Consider Possible Actions
7. Choose and Act on Choice" (Heller Levitt & Hartwig Moorhead, 2013, p. 215).

Dagmar Fenner suggests **the** following steps. (Fenner, 2020, p. 80f):

Step 1: Situation analysis: Descriptive level

The first step is to analyze the action situation on a *descriptive level* and to clarify what it is all about. All facts and data relevant to the decision should be collected and all information critically examined.

Step 2: Interest and conflict *analysis*

Again, on a descriptive level, all persons or groups of persons involved in a moral conflict are then listed and their different expectations, interests, and claims named. Without premature prejudice, the perspectives and positions of all those involved are to be noted and perceived in a context-sensitive manner in their respective historical, cultural, or social backgrounds or their diverse networks of dependencies and influences.

Step 3: Analysis of the alternative courses of action

At this point at the latest experience and creative imagination need to be used to list all alternative courses of action in the specific decision-making situation. Except in emergency situations there are usually a lot more than just two possibilities, so the decision-making process should be taken away from a simple "either-or"-decision, and small-scale intermediate solutions should be taken into account. It must also be clarified what means are actually available to implement the individual options and what consequences of action are to be expected in each case.

*Step 4: Analysis of values and norms: Normative Leve*l

The fourth step takes us on to a normative level, because the individual options for action must now be assessed in terms of the relevant ethical values and norms. Using the persons and groups of persons identified in Step 2, the ethical arguments for and against certain alternatives can be listed. In doing so, it is important to uncover the normative ideas underlying the individual arguments and to examine the extent to which the individual norms, principles, or rights can be justified or must be criticized.

Step 5: Interest and conflict analysis

After critically reflecting all ethical arguments and weighing the values and norms on which they are based ideally it would be possible to determine the best possible option for action. The important thing here is to take the impartial standpoint of morality or *objective standpoint of morality* so that the assessment will also be impartial and can claim universal validity. Often, the solution is the choice of the lesser evil for all concerned or a fair distribution of benefits and burdens.

Similarly, the **model of ethical decision-making according to Bleisch, Huppenbauer & Baumberger** (2021) which aims at providing a systematic guide to ethical decision-making and a practical framework for structuring arguments and discussion consists of:

1 Step : Analysis of the actual state
2 Step : Formulating the moral question
3 Step : Analysis of the arguments
4 Step : Evaluation and decision
5 Step : Implementation.

Finally, some guiding questions can be identified whose core content can be found in one wording or another within various models and instruments for ethical decision-making – for example, in **M. J. Úriz Pemán and F. Idareta Goldaracena** (see ibid., 2017):

1. "Describir la cuestión o el dilema ético:
   - ¿Quién está implicado? ¿Cuál es su implicación?
   - ¿Qué tiene el dilema?
   - ¿Qué implicaciones tiene? ¿Qué riesgos hay?
   - ¿Cuáles son las características principales?
   - ¿Qué tipo de asunto es?
2. considerar los aspectos éticos y jurídicos:
   - Considera todas las directrices éticas y normas jurídicas.
   - Identifica tus propios valores personales pertinentes para el asunto.
   - Identifica los valores sociales o comunitarios pertinentes para el asunto.
   - Identifica los estándares profesionales pertinentes.
   - Identifica las leyes y regulaciones pertinentes.
   - Aplica estas directrices.
3. examinar todos los conflictos:
   - Describe los conflictos que experimentas internamente.
   - Describe los conflictos que experimentas y que son externos (implican a nosotros, usuarios, supervisor, profesional, etc.).
   - Decide cuáles de estos conflictos son menos importantes (si el externo prima sobre el interno, si puedes minimizar alguno de ellos...).
4. Resolver los conflictos pidiendo ayuda, si la necesitas, para tomar la decisión:
   - onsulta con otros colegas, expertos o supervisores.
   - Consulta bibliografía profesional pertinente.
   - Busca ayuda en organizaciones profesionales o comités de ética.
5. generar todos los posibles cursos de acción.
6. examinar y evaluar las alternativas de actuación (se intenta priorizar entre alternativas)
   - Considera las preferencias de las personas usuarias y de las otras personas implicadas desde una comprensión total de sus valores y creencias éticas (p.e.: autonomía del usuario).
   - Elimina las alternativas que sean incompatibles con los valores y creencias de la persona usuaria y de otras personas significativas implicadas en el caso (no intentes imponer tus propios valores).
   - Elimina las alternativas que sean incompatibles con otras normativas relevantes pertinentes en el caso.
   - Elimina las alternativas para las que no tienes apoyo ni recursos (sé realista).
   - Elimina las alternativas que no se ajusten a los principios éticos de universalidad, publicidad y justicia.
   - Con el propósito de auxiliar en este paso, P. Kenyon recoge las siguientes preguntas sobre la universalidad: ¿La acción es aplicable a todas las personas en situaciones similares (incluyéndote a ti mismo/a)? ¿Recomendarías actuar así a otros profesionales? ¿Lo aprobarías si un colega lo hiciera?

- En relación a la publicidad señala las siguientes: ¿La acción se basa en estándares éticos reconocidos por todas las personas implicadas? ¿Explicarías esa acción a tus colegas o en público? ¿Aceptarían ellos esa explicación?
- Y con respecto a la justicia: ¿La acción trata a las personas justamente? ¿Harías lo mismo con otros usuarios en situación similar? ¿Harías lo mismo si la persona usuaria fuera conocida o influyente?
- Prevé las posibles consecuencias de las alternativas aceptables que te quedan (a corto y largo plazo; ciertas, probables, improbables, etc.).
- Prioriza las alternativas aceptables que te quedan.
- Para ayudar en este paso, Kenyon (1998) recoge las preguntas que proponen Loewenberg y Dolgoff (1982): ¿Qué alternativas protegen más los derechos y bienestar de los usuarios y de otras personas? ¿Qué alternativas protegen más los derechos e intereses de la sociedad? ¿Qué puedes hacer para minimizar los conflictos entre proteger derechos y bienestar de los usuarios, la sociedad, otros, etc.? ¿Qué alternativa causa "el menor daño" posible?

7. seleccionar y evaluar la actuación elegida (el mejor curso de acción):
   - Especialmente si no hemos elegido la acción que estaba situada en primer lugar, tenemos que evaluar nuestra decisión, preguntándonos también si estamos siendo influidos por algún factor que no hubiéramos reconocido o si debiéramos reconsiderar algo.
8. planificar la actuación: Desarrolla un plan de actuación y llévalo a cabo.
9. Evaluar el resultado de la acción que has llevado a cabo:
   - ¿Los resultados eran los esperados? ¿Aún piensas que ésa era la mejor decisión?
10. examinar las consecuencias/implicaciones:
    - ¿Qué has aprendido del proceso y sus resultados? ¿Qué implicaciones tiene para futuras tomas de decisiones éticas?".[3]

3 - 1. "Describe the ethical issue or dilemma:
- Who is involved, what is their involvement?
- What is the dilemma?
- What are the implications? What are the risks?
- What are the main features?
- What kind of issue is it?
- 2. Consider ethical and legal aspects:
- Consider all ethical guidelines and legal standards.
- Identify your own personal values relevant to the issue.
- Identify social or community values relevant to the issue.
- Identify relevant professional standards.
- Identify relevant laws and regulations.
- Apply these guidelines.
- 3. Examine all conflicts:
- Describe conflicts you experience internally.
- Describe the conflicts you experience that are external (involving us, users, supervisor, professional, etc.).
- Decide which of these conflicts are less important (if the external one takes precedence over the internal one, if you can minimise any of them...).
- 4. Resolve the conflicts by asking for help, if you need it, to make the decision:
- Consult with other colleagues, experts or supervisors.
- Consult relevant professional literature.
- Seek help from professional organisations or ethics committees.

SAMBA aims at meeting these expectations. At the same time, SAMBA strives for compact and concise lightness, and argumentative elegance in the struggle for the ethically right and the ethically good, and thus to contributing to a better world.

- 5. Generate all possible courses of action.
- 6. Examine and evaluate alternative courses of action (attempts to prioritise between alternatives).
- Consider the preferences of clients and significant others with a full understanding of their values and ethical beliefs (e.g., client autonomy).
- Eliminate alternatives that are incompatible with the values and beliefs of the client and significant others involved in the case (do not try to impose your own values).
- Eliminate alternatives that are incompatible with other relevant regulations relevant to the case.
- Eliminate alternatives for which you have no support or resources (be realistic).
- Eliminate alternatives that do not conform to the ethical principles of universality, publicity and fairness.
- In order to assist in this step, P. Kenyon collects the following questions on universality: Is the action applicable to all people in similar situations (including yourself)? Would you recommend this action to other professionals? Would you approve if a colleague did it?
- With regard to publicity: Is the action based on ethical standards recognised by all persons involved? Would you explain the action to your colleagues or in public? Would they accept the explanation?
- And with regard to fairness: Does the action treat people fairly? Would you do the same for other users in a similar situation? Would you do the same if the user were known or infamous?
- Anticipate the possible consequences of the remaining acceptable alternatives (short and long term; certain, probable, improbable, etc.).
- Prioritise the remaining acceptable alternatives.
- To help you in this step, Kenyon (1998) takes up the questions proposed by Loewenberg and Dolgoff (1982): Which alternatives best protect the rights and welfare of users and others? Which alternatives best protect the rights and interests of society? What can you do to minimise conflicts between protecting the rights and welfare of users, society, others, etc.? Which alternative causes "the least harm" possible?
- 7. select and evaluate the chosen action (the best course of action):
- Especially if we have not chosen the action that was placed first, we need to evaluate our decision, also asking ourselves if we are being influenced by any factors that we would not have recognised or if we should reconsider something.
- 8. Plan the action: Develop an action plan and carry it out.
- 9. Evaluate the outcome of the action you have taken:
- Were the results as expected, and do you still think this was the best decision?
- 10. Examine the consequences/implications:
- What have you learned from the process and its outcomes? What implications does it have for future ethical decision-making?"

2 Ethics in a Global Context

Summary

This chapter addresses the question of how ethics can be successful and convincing in a global context. For this, respect for freedom and human dignity of all people is necessary – the two principles of all principles of ethics. Because if all human beings are understood as free and as bearers of human dignity, one must not impose an unjustifiable ought on them, which would mean a violation or an instrumentalization. Rather, the two principles of all principles, freedom and human dignity, and respect of the plurality of ethics require an ethical justification i.e. "good reasons".

At the same time, the two principles of all principles freedom and human dignity form preconditions for the possibility of perception, consideration, reflection, and an ethically justifiable and legitimate handling of the plurality of ethics because even thinking of it, talking about it, or practicing plurality of ethics lives on the presupposition of the sources of the plurality of ethics: freedom and human dignity of all people.

In the course of ethical decision-making one repeatedly encounters geographical categories (such as west/east, global/local...) that suggest a normative justification for a statement or position that relates to a particular geographically defined place or area, e.g. either for or against freedom and human dignity of all people. In this regard, one of the fundamental questions is what relevance geographical categories may have in an ethical discourse. Of course, historical backgrounds, context, place, and time, etc., influence ways of thinking and opinions. However, if in the course of ethical decision-making, the argument is based only on place or time of origin, its normative validity and argumentative power must be questioned. Because these geographical categories always remain relative to the starting point, which is relevant because they are geographical categories according to their content. The question arises where this point of view was taken from and how it was determined that one place is in the "east" and another in the "west." For example, Vienna is "east" of Lucerne, but in the normal use of the two categories in the human rights discourse, Vienna would probably be assigned to the "West." These categories seem to be based on racist thinking, because they suggest that people in a particular context are different in regards to freedom and human dignity from people outside this context and that freedom and human dignity are only about perceptible differences.

This world forms the global context in which ethics is to be thought. In this context the demands on ethics are also expressed in particular terms with regard to the plurality of ethics to be respected. The above-mentioned need for ethics *first* represents an expression of respect for the freedom and human dignity of all human beings – *the two principles of all principles of ethics.* If all human beings are understood as free and as bearers of human dignity, then one must not impose on them an unjustified ought, which would mean a violation of their freedom or an instrumentalization. Rather, the *two principles of all principles freedom and human dignity* require an ethical justification – "good reasons". ("Good reasons" means that it must be conceivable that all human beings in their effective freedom and autonomy as well as in their full equality would agree to these reasons –

within a model of thought and not within a real worldwide referendum – on ethical grounds (see Kirchschlaeger, 2021a).

Second, at the same time the need for rational arguments as an expression of respect for the plurality of ethics is to be met with "good reasons".

Moreover, the *two principles of all principles freedom and human dignity* prove to be pre*conditions for the possibility* of perception, consideration, reflection, and ethically justifiable and legitimate handling of the plurality of ethics since already thinking of, speaking about, let alone practicing plurality of ethics lives from the presupposition of the sources of the plurality of ethics: freedom and human dignity of all human beings. Otherwise, how could all the voices – especially in a global context – that have been calling for the plurality of ethics be heard at all if they were denied their existence or their right to exist? How else should a recognition of the plurality of voices take place, if these voices would neither be allowed to sound nor be heard? How else should the plurality of ethics emerge and be lived if coercion and oppression were to erase its origin and if, instead of a circle of moral community conceived as inclusive as possible and equal a bottleneck of exclusion and dominance were to propagate uniformity? In other words: plurality of ethics – in particular the equal recognition of all this plurality of ethics as well as its lived theory and practice – are based on the *two principles of all principles freedom and human dignity* as pre*conditions for their possibility*.

This already implies that plurality of ethics neither leads to arbitrariness or relativism, nor to an "anything goes"-attitude, but knows and strives for ethical statements and positional references with binding force – if only because the plurality of ethics would otherwise be cutting off the branch on which the plurality of ethics itself is sitting on.

Finally, relativism and "anything goes" reach the limits of their argumentative persuasiveness when we consider thoroughly what they actually stand for in the final analysis: relativism or "anything goes" would be tantamount to saying that even positions, statements, or actions which – even against the background of different ethical traditions, cultures, beliefs, approaches, models, schools, and currents – are clearly to be described as ethically wrong or ethically bad (e.g. not understanding individuals or certain people as human beings or sexual violence against children) would supposedly be understood as ethically right and good, because then everything would need to be regarded as ethically right and good. However, there are no "good reasons" for ethical approval of such positions, statements, or actions.

Ethics in a global context also encounters two main objections that need to be reflected upon:

1. Time and again people in all corners of this world tried at different times to prevent individuals or groups of people from being human, from having freedom and human dignity, as well as from having human rights that protect human dignity or from having individual human rights. In order to support these attempts argumentatively, arguments and reasons come into play that can be identified

as "Ten Argumentation Patterns of Exclusion" (see Kirchschlaeger, 2016d, pp. 170-178). These occur everywhere on earth and in all conceivable discourses whenever attempts at excluding freedom and human dignity from individuals or groups of people are undertaken.

The starting point for the discovery of the "Ten Argumentation Patterns of Exclusion" was the examination of the case study of the women's suffrage debate in Switzerland. Women's suffrage exists in the whole of Switzerland only since 1990. It was adopted by a narrow two-thirds majority in most parts of the country on February 7, 1971 – also very late by international standards. But it took until March 25, 1990 for Swiss women to be recognized as voters in the whole of Switzerland. It was not until the Swiss Federal Supreme Court ruled in favor of a complaint filed by women from Appenzell Innerrhoden and confirmed the unconstitutionality of the Innerrhoden cantonal constitution on this point that women were also granted the right to vote in the canton of Appenzell Innerrhoden. Based on this Federal Court decision, women's suffrage was introduced at the cantonal level in the canton of Appenzell Innerrhoden on November 27, 1990 – against the majority of the electorate – making it the last canton in Switzerland to introduce women's suffrage. (see Neue Zuercher Zeitung, 2011)

At that time, the following ten arguments against women's suffrage were listed, all of which – it should be noted at the outset – prove to be ethically unacceptable:

1. *the role intended for women as individuals by the collective – that of a mother – would not be able to be linked to politics;*
2. *the contribution of women as individuals to the collective, in the sense of "society depends on women without voting rights to function, to evolve, and to survive."*
3. *a change would open the door to what is rejected by the majority in society and labelled "as evil" – in the case of women's suffrage in Switzerland, it was argued that women's suffrage would bring Bolshevism to Switzerland* (see Gariup, 2011);
4. *the presumed self-image of women themselves, in the sense of: "if you asked the women, they would not want to participate in politics at all";*
5. *the perceived lack of skills necessary for women to exercise this human right;*
6. *one's tradition and culture, in the sense of: "This corresponds to our tradition and culture" or "This is our tradition and culture" or "We are a special case – and that is good and should remain so";*
7. *one's history, in the sense of "We've always done it that way";*
8. *one's history as a model of success, in the sense of: "We have fared very well so far";*
9. *sovereignty, in the sense of "This is our business";*
10. *internal cohesion against outside influences: "We won't let anyone tell us what to do".*

These ten arguments appeared in different combinations and sequences in the democratic opinion-forming and decision-making processes of the time.

They find their counterarguments, *first,* in the justification of freedom and human dignity of all people and human rights based on the principle of vulnerability (see Kirchschlaeger, 2013e, 2015b, 2016b).

Second, the counter-argument of the reversal of the burden of proof can help to invalidate these ten arguments. In the course of the reversal of the burden of proof, "good reasons" ("good reasons" means that it must be conceivable that all people in their effective freedom and autonomy as well as in their full equality would agree to these reasons (within a model of thought and not within a real worldwide referendum) on ethical grounds) (see Kirchschlaeger, 2021a) are demanded from the counterpart in the discourse which would speak for the respective argument. It will most likely be difficult to find corresponding "good reasons" for these ten arguments.

Third, the following observation weakens the persuasiveness of the ten arguments. Regardless of whether a state is talked about because of its attacks on freedom, human dignity, and human rights, whether a religious practice that goes against freedom or is inhumane is named in a particular context or whether discrimination against women is being discussed in a dialogue with a religious community: these ten arguments seem to come up in the same or similar way across religions, worldviews and states when, from a particular position, an attempt is made in a self-interest to restrict or deny freedom, human dignity, all their human rights or individual specific human rights to all people, a certain group of people or individuals. The point here is not to prove empirically that these ten arguments of exclusion are always and everywhere used in situations where freedom, human dignity, all human rights or specific human rights are restricted or denied. Rather, it needs to be questioned whether these ten arguments of exclusion are not used in each case or whether their respective scheme is not recognizable.

These two questions weaken the ten arguments of exclusion insofar as their supposedly strong contextual reference, essential for the argument, the same or similar arguments of exclusion are also used in other contexts, where other people are deprived of their freedom, their human dignity and their human rights. The main reasons for the ten arguments of exclusion – namely, one's collective understanding, one's state, one's culture, tradition, religion, worldview, one's value system, one's history, one's sovereignty – lose their persuasive power when it becomes clear that the same arguments are used by other states, cultures, traditions, religions, worldviews, civilizations, value systems, etc. This means that it is not one's own system which is the cause of exclusion. This means that it is not the uniqueness of one's own position that is the decisive factor for exclusion, but something that transcends states, religions, and worldviews. Thus, the arguments at least start to waver. For example, it is no longer "typically Swiss" to deny women their right to vote, but something that certain circles in Switzerland, but also circles not in Switzerland – independent of the Swiss state, Swiss context Swiss history, Swiss tradition, Swiss values, etc. – promote. This means that these ten arguments are actually not based on the uniqueness of one's own, but on something else. Consequently, they build on something else than what has been primarily claimed by the counterpart in the discourse.

Fourth, these questions about what transcends states, religions, and worldviews expose the probably more applicable reasons of the arguments of exclusion, which are less dependent on the context. The reasons for the arguments of exclusion, which are less dependent on the context, culture, tradition, religion, worldview, value system, history, etc., but rather on a different unifying factor that is not relative to states, religions or worldviews. This unifying factor is apparently characterized by a basic conservative orientation – apparently because a basic conservative orientation is associated with freedom, human dignity, human rights, and the rule of law, or because a conformity with freedom, human dignity and human rights of a collective can be preserved in the conservative sense.

This unifying factor characterizes racism and that which has been clearly refuted scientifically, which is to be covered up with the reference to what is supposedly "one's own" – with a "smoke screen" as it were, so as not let the real reasons come to light.

This unifying factor, however, provokes the need to dispel the probably not entirely unjustified suspicion that one's own culture, tradition, religion, worldview, value system, history, sovereignty, etc., is being twisted to suit the particular interests of specific people or a specific group. And it can arguably be called illiberal in that its opposition to respecting freedom, human dignity and human rights or the willingness to negate freedom, human dignity and human rights for all people or for individuals, or to accept that people lose their freedom, human dignity and human rights completely or to a certain extent.

Or the ten arguments of exclusion could go back to the claim to sovereignty and power of certain individuals and groups in a collective. If this cannot be refuted by the counterpart in the discourse, powerful people and decision-makers of states or of religious and ideological communities can be exposed in their actually decisive particular interests or institutional-political considerations in view of the use of these ten argumentation figures of exclusion (see Langan, 1982, pp. 31-34).

Fifth, the non-existent content-related divergence of one's culture, tradition, religion, worldview, one's value system, one's history, one's religious or worldview-based traditions, convictions, and teachings on freedom, human dignity, and human rights are obvious, which also explains the reasons why a contextually based undermining of freedom, human dignity, and human rights ceases to exist.

Sixth, the preoccupation with the ten arguments of exclusion and the resulting contradictions and debunkings gives rise to possible credibility and coherence problems and of declining effectiveness or persuasiveness of the respective collective vis-à-vis people inside and outside the respective community. Often, anti-freedom and anti-human dignity thinking and acting, as well as human rights violations, pressure, coercion, violence, and extremism, in or by a collective can be signs of its weakness and gradual decline in its importance. Or to put it another way: why force people to do something if you can convince them to do something?

Seventh, the examination of the ten arguments of exclusion, which also perceives the resistance and opposition to exclusion in individual states and religious and worldview-based communities, reveals that neither states nor religious and worldview-based communities represent homogeneous, monolithic, precisely definable, and graspable entities that remain eternally the same, endlessly existing and unchanging. Rather, they are highly complex, and heterogeneous (e.g., conservative, liberal, and other currents), where change and transformation happens (e.g., developments, progress, and others), with foundations, growth, and demises, as well as contributions and resistances to the historical emergence of freedom, human dignity, and human rights. In their past, their present, and probably also in their future, states as well as religious and worldview-based communities know diversity, differences, internal discourses, differences of opinion, frictions, and a competition of arguments and reasons – probably at different levels of openness, intensity and publicity. Marks in preserved oral and written traditions bear witness to such processes.

For example, voices calling for human rights in states and religious and worldview-based communities can be heard when there is oppression, fighting, and annihilation of minorities, a clash of power of the collective against the powerlessness of the individual, injustice, conflicts between socioeconomic groups, etc. Concrete issues, problems, challenges, and historical experiences of injustice and violation that affect essential elements and areas of human existence that human beings need to survive and live as human beings trigger human rights-based opposition. For all human beings are and remain bearers of freedom, human dignity and human rights within and outside of state, religious and worldview-based collectives.

Eighth, there is a tendency to see and make the differences between states and religious and worldview-based communities greater than they actually are. "Societies change faster than foreigners' pictures of them. [...] It is true that different parts of the world have sometimes had radically different histories, which still exert an influence on their vocabularies, their ways of thinking, their religions, their values. But the influences on the members of virtually all societies are now much more a mix of local and global than they were even a hundred years ago" (Griffin, 2015, p. 562).

2. In the course of ethical decision making one repeatedly encounters *geographic categories (such as west/east, global/local...)* that suggest a normative justification for a statement or position that relates to a particular geographically defined place or area, e.g., either for or against freedom and human dignity of all people. However, these categories raise doubts about their epistemic significance for the following reasons:

a. The question arises as to how relevant geographical categories may be in an ethical discourse. Of course, historical background, context, place, and time etc. have an influence on ways of thinking and opinions. The normative validity and argumentative power of the latter must be questioned, however, if in the course of ethical decision-making the argumentation is based only on place or time of origin.
b. These geographical categories always remain relative to the starting point, which is important, because they are geographical categories based on their content. The question arises where this point of view was taken from and how it was determined that one place is in the "East" and another in the "West". For example, Vienna is "east" of Lucerne, but in the normal use of the two categories in a human rights discourse, Vienna would probably be assigned to the "West."
c. Categories such as East/West are based on the assumption or construction of supposedly definable, tangible, monolithic, homogeneous, eternally existing, unchanging, opposing, and separate worlds. It seems clear what comprises the so-called "West" or "East" and what traditions, principles, and values these two parts of the world are based on.
d. It turns out that it is difficult, if not impossible, to understand these categories – for example, the so-called "East" and "West" – and their respective values on which these two categories are based. If one attempts to develop a comprehensive definition of the so-called "West" and "East" and to assume that one knows the values on which they are based, then one has to be careful given the prevailing plurality, heterogeneity, and dynamism in the "East" or "West". An epistemological approach would probably fail because these categories cannot be defined, apart from their designation as geographical positions. Reality is much more complex and the supposedly categorizing values – for example, in the geographic "East" and "West" – turn out to be irrelevant because of the religious and worldview-based plurality and heterogeneity, normative diversity, and different legal and political systems, as well as great differences in economic power.
e. The schematization contained in these categories, based on the assumption and construction of supposedly definable, comprehensive, monolithic, homogeneous, eternal, unchanging, separate, and contradictory worlds (e.g. "East"/ "West", ...), is an oversimplification. It reduces the diversity contained in such categories, which is very important for shaping the discussion. The two supposed poles turn out to be diverse and heterogeneous in their internal structure and contain different currents (e.g. conservative, liberal, etc.). This would be important for the subjects of the respective discourse when using

these categories. This kind of schematization, with its notion of monolithic, definable, comprehensive, homogeneous, eternal, and unchanging internal structures, suppresses the epistemically necessary perception and consideration of different bases, developments, and the dynamics of change.

f. On this basis, the categories "East" or "West" are used in the argumentation, for example in the following sentence: "Because freedom and human dignity originated in the 'West', they do not apply in the 'East'." Apart from the relevance of temporal and local circumstances for the validity of universal norms discussed in the following section, the categories "East" and "West" establish a normative statement ("freedom and human dignity do not apply in the 'East'").
g. An argument based on these categories assumes incorrectly that the "West" possesses a certain superior quality that the "East" lacks. The statement "because freedom and human dignity originated in the 'West'..." also contains the assumption that the "West" supposedly possesses a power of innovation and creativity that the "East" allegedly does not have (see Frezzo, 2015).
h. Assigning content to a particular geographical location or area is not convincing, because a particular content A or tendency B can be found in what we call the "East" as well as in what we call the "West," and the contradictory position C or tendency D can also be found everywhere (see Joas, 2015, p. 78). These patterns of argumentation on which positions or trends are based do not depend primarily on their geographical or temporal origin, as such schematization would like to suggest. Rather, it is a liberal position that can be found in all places and all points of the compass, as can its counter-positions. Liberal and illiberal positions exist independently of longitude and latitude. When a geographical reference is made to a particular place – for example, in statements such as "in the East they think this way" or "in the West they do it that way" – there is a danger that "in the East" or "in the West" becomes an argument that ignores everything else, especially the real reasons and factors. In doing so, the argument may hinder the examination of the real reasons and factors for qualifying as "good reasons" – which means that it must be conceivable that all people in their real freedom and autonomy, as well as in their full equality would agree to these reasons – within a model of thought and not within a real worldwide referendum – on ethical grounds (see Kirchschlaeger, 2021a). However, this critical examination would be necessary with regard to the normative validity and argumentative power of the real reasons and factors.
i. These categories seem to be based on racist thinking, because they suggest that people in a certain context can be different in freedom and human dignity from people outside that context and that freedom and human dignity are only about perceptible differences.

3 Ethics and Law

Summary

This chapter focuses on the relationship between ethics and law in order to gain a precise understanding of the field of ethics – ethical decisions in contrast to socially normed decisions based on social acceptance as well as in contrast to legal decisions with reference to valid law created by judicial decisions.
The relationship between ethics and law shapes the following possibilities of norms:

- Laws without ethical content that can only be described as legal (such as the right of way in road traffic);
- Laws with ethical content that can be described as legal and legitimate (e.g., the prohibition of murder);
- ethical norms without the character of law, which can only be described as legitimate (e.g. donating to the needy);
- Laws that are legal but illegitimate (e.g., current provisions in asylum and migration law that violate freedom, human dignity, and human rights)

Due to the risk that positive law could also include illegitimate norms,

- because the democratic opinion-forming and decision-making process has not been fair;
- because ethical problems arising later in the legal practice were not foreseen in the course of the legislation;
- because there was a lack of political will to take ethical considerations sufficiently into account in the democratic opinion-forming and decision-making process, or the latter did not find a majority;
- because thanks to greater financial resources one position has enjoyed much more public and media exposure than another, resulting in one-sided legislation that unfairly serves certain special interests;

the law and legal practice to prevent illegitimate laws need to be continuously critically examined for their moral foundation through ethics, in order to be and remain not only legal but also legitimate. In this regard, the *two principles of all principles of ethics* freedom and human dignity, as well as human rights that protect freedom and human dignity play an important role in their effect on law where they lay the foundation and set the framework for positive law.

The relevance and quality of ethical decision-making processes are enhanced not only by a clear view of their necessity and desirability and a critical knowledge of their content and methodological possibilities, but also by a precise delineation of their field of work.

A first differentiation in this regard draws the line between ethical decision-making processes and socially standardized decisions. While ethical decisions claim to be ethically binding and strive for validity on the basis of ethical justification, social decisions only need social acceptance to claim validity. However, this social acceptance says nothing about their legitimacy. In other words socially accepted decisions can also be ethically unacceptable, which leads to the fact that ethics as a science must critically examine the legitimacy of socially supported decisions.

A further differentiation is made by determining the multi-layered relationship between law and ethics and their impact on ethical decision-making processes. Legal decisions are made within valid law which in its validity goes back to judicial decisions. The genesis of positive law in liberal constitutional states goes back to democratic opinion-forming and decision-making processes. Ethical decisions in such democratic opinion-forming and decision-making processes can lead to the creation of legal norms. This potential binding force in positive law must be taken into account in ethical decisions. Positive law represents a system of positive coercive norms as a formal regulation according to the principle of equality of the "external" actions of people of a political community with the aim of peaceful coexistence (see Pieper, 2017, p. 111). It forms a binding order for all social action, which knows enforcement mechanisms and sanctions.

Positive law should be based on morality and ethics as a condition of its legitimacy and right to exist (e.g., the liberal-democratic legal system is based on the recognition of freedom, justice, and equality as unconditional values). Law can be understood as an indirect expression of morality. Its justification should be the positive right through ethics in order to maintain the relationship between laws and ethical norms. This is significant in that

- there are laws without ethical content that can only be described as legal (such as the right of way in road traffic);
- there are laws with ethical content that can be described as legal and legitimate (e.g. the prohibition of murder);
- there are ethical norms without the character of law, which can only be described as legitimate (e.g. donating to the needy);
- there are laws that are legal but illegitimate (e.g., current provisions in asylum and migration law that violate freedom, human dignity, and the rule of law, human dignity and human rights.)

Positive law always runs the risk of including illegitimate norms,

- because the democratic opinion-forming and decision-making process has not been fair;
- because ethical problems arising later in legal practice were not foreseen in the course of the legislation;
- because there was a lack of political will to take ethical considerations sufficiently into account in the democratic opinion-forming and decision-making process, or the latter did not find a majority;
- because thanks to greater financial resources one position has enjoyed much more public and media exposure than another, resulting in one-sided legislation that unfairly serves certain special interests.

In order to prevent as much as possible the possibility that there might be laws that could be described as legal and illegitimate, positive law and the practice of law depend on the continuous critical examination of their moral foundation through ethics. This entails the need for justifying legal norms through ethics as the "common thread" of the relationship between ethics and law.

There are different levels in the relationship between ethics and law: on the level of justification, moral rights prove to be justified when they correspond with a justified moral duty for which "good reasons" (as introduced above under 1.1 Need for Ethical Decisions) can be named and thus the principle of generalizability is fulfilled. Legal rights then formulate legitimate and legal claims of the members of the legal system as part of a positive legal order. Potential perpetrators who violate moral rights only have to fear internal sanctions such as moral feelings (shame, indignation, guilt). These are based on the fact that the moral concept serving as a foundation for moral feelings is shared. In the case of a violation of legal rights, external sanctions await the offender(s), which do not depend on the conviction of the parties involved and are imposed and implemented by a state authority with enforcement power. Such an authority is absent in the case of moral rights.

In addition to this distinction between legality and legitimacy, another difference with regard to its enforcement between positive law and ethics becomes clear in the following: "Someone can act completely correctly legally and yet immorally; however, only a breach of law is punished, not a violation of moral norms." (Pieper, 2017, p. 118) The moral community and a critical public can watch over the enforcement of moral rights and demand respect for them.

Particularly the differences in the area of sanctions and the instance enforcing them as well as the associated lack of legitimate coercion that would ensure their enforcement lead to moral rights being referred to as "weak rights".

Moral rights form human constructions that derive from reciprocal unconditional moral duties. They are part of a morality which, as a system of obligations, includes different kinds of obligations (asymmetrical, conditional, unconditional). Reciprocal obligations alone cannot turn subjects and objects of these obligations into bearers of rights. It needs a willful decision for those rights to be endowed.

At this point, the question arises how this juridification can be justified, i.e. why people are bearers of rights. Legal justification knows the limit of its relevance within the boundaries of the national legal system. This limitation is to be dissolved in the case of moral rights because in the case of moral rights the principle of generalizability has to be fulfilled. Conversely, the justification of moral rights is not dependent on the justification on a legal level, because the legal level is based on a legitimation that is limited in its validity.

The justification of moral rights is also invoked when, for example, human rights are created as positive rights in order to critically review this process. At this point, we need to preemptively dispel a potential misunderstanding: it does not mean that rights that pass this scrutiny are automatically positive. Because when transforming them into positive law political and historical influences also come into play.

The transformation of moral rights into positive law gives the following advantages (Alexy, 1998, pp. 244-264):

1. Positive law results in improved chances of enforcement. In conjunction with this, the risks for unfair advantages arising from immoral behavior might increase.
2. Positivization can solve problems of interpretation and concretization that arise from the abstract nature of moral rights through regulated and controllable legal decision making.
3. The duties corresponding with moral rights lead in the course of a positivization of these rights to the constitution of state organizations capable of taking on these duties.

Transforming moral rights into positive law does not turn out to be morally necessary, however, because there is no obligation to do so from an ethical perspective, since moral rights are self-sufficient in this respect and do not draw on sources outside themselves. It is, however, possible that it is done out of a moral obligation (see Tugendhat, 1993, p. 350) or based on a rational self-interest of the participants (see Lohmann, 1998, pp. 62-95).

Morally relevant is only the decision which legal system the positivization is based on or which legal system represents a part of the result of this positivization process. This must fulfil the requirements of the moral rights.

During the positivization of moral rights by a democratic opinion-forming and decision-making process in a constitutional state it leads to "abstraction and exoneration of positive law vis-à-vis morality" (Lohmann, 1998, p. 90) in the Kantian sense: the individual is freed from the obligation to be moral to the authenticity of his or her individual and self-responsible way of life, which can be moral (see Lohmann, 1998, p. 90).

Positive law does not only draw on ethics in the justification of its fundamental pillars. In its enforcement the law is dependent on a corresponding ethos. For realizing positive law, a corresponding moral consciousness is needed. Rights are respected not only because their violation results in sanctions, but mostly because a morality associated with them dictates that the law be observed. Martin Luther King formulated this in his speech "Facing the Challenge of a New Age" at the NAAACP Emancipation Day Rally on January 1, 1957 in Atlanta as follows: "I know that there are those who say that this can't be done through the courts, it can't be done through laws, you can't legislate morals. They would say that integration must come by education not legislation. Well, I choose to be dialectical at that point. It's not either law or education. It's both legislation and education" (Luther King, 1957).

Finally, the *two principles of all principles of ethics* freedom, and human dignity as well as human rights protecting freedom and human dignity have an effect on law. Freedom, human dignity, and human rights not only make up the framework for positive law but also for its emergence in the course of a democratic process of opinion-forming and decision-making as well as a basic condition for its legitimacy. "Modern legal culture moves in a peculiar tension, almost a contradiction: more and more it is determined by an empirical or rather pragmatic thinking, but it recognizes moral principles which, like human rights, are characterized by a categorical binding force and which, for this very reason, do not bow to empirical-pragmatic thinking. Human rights have the meaning of categorical principles of law and as such form a counterpoint in modern legal culture" (Hoeffe, 1990, p. 11). The categorical principles of law create preconditions and framework conditions so that diversity can also become a reality, so that legitimate diversity can also be created in the face of resistance (see Hoeffe, 1990, p. 11). Within ethics freedom, human dignity, and human rights play a special role in the interaction between ethics and law which is characterized by the fact that ethics can be cast in law and law is dependent on ethical justification and needs the continuous critical ethical review to be and remain not only legal but also legitimate.

4 Human Ethical Decisions Are and Will Remain in Demand – Also in the Future

Summary

In this chapter, you can expect a discussion of the possibility of delegating ethical decisions to so-called so called "artificial intelligence" to lessen the burden on humans. The focus is on the question of whether machines have moral capability or not, and whether humans can entrust them with ethical decisions based on their ethical decision-making capacities. In the following will be shown that this is not possible due to the lack of vulnerability, conscience, freedom, responsibility, and autonomy in machines as well the absence of moral capability , also in the forseeable future. Ethical decisions are and remain an exclusive responsibility of human beings. Only human beings can recognize what is ethically legitimate and decide and act accordingly.

4.1 Delegating Ethical Decisions to Machines?

The rapid pace of technological progress raises the question of whether ethical decisions could not be delegated to so-called so called "artificial intelligence" (AI) to relieve the burden on humans (see Anderson & Anderson, 2011, pp. 1-4). This is argued by the fact that "AI systems, due to their increasing intelligence, autonomy and interaction capabilities, are increasingly perceived and expected as moral agents" (Dignum, 2019, p. 36). Terms such as "moral technologies", which are used in the current discourse about digitization, automation, machinization, robotization, and the use of so called "artificial intelligence", suggest such an option. They express the expectation that it would be possible to create "moral technologies". The term "moral technologies" refers to their abilities to follow ethical rules, make moral decisions and to perform actions on that basis. The term "moral technologies" expresses the desire to create machines with ethical principles and standards. This would be achieved through programming, but mainly through training and learning.

Talking of "moral technologies" raises questions. Can technical inventions be moral? Can so called "artificial intelligence" be ethical? Can technological systems possess moral capability? Can we ascribe to them the ability to make ethical decisions (see Sullins, 2006)? Or do they possess a limited but not complete morality like a "functional morality" (Wallach & Allen, 2009, p. 39) that allows them to assess the ethical consequences of their actions, or a mindless morality without acquiring the qualities that humans possess as a basis for their morality (see Floridi & Sanders, 2004)? Or is it impossible to think of technologies with morality? In the following, the characterization as "moral technologies", which are supposed to have moral capability, will be discussed from an ethical point of view concerning possibly delegating ethical decisions to machines. We will focus on the question of whether machines have moral capability and whether humans can delegate ethical decisions to them.

4.2 Vulnerability

"Moral technologies" and "ethical artificial intelligence" are first of all confronted with one of the peculiarities of the moral capability that distinguishes humans from machines and so called "artificial intelligence": the vulnerability of humans in connection with their "first-person perspective" and their "self-relation". The term "vulnerability" (see Kirchschlaeger, 2013a, pp. 241-267) encompasses the possibility of being attacked or injured and, at the same time, the lack of ability or means to extricate oneself from this situation and protect oneself from injury (see Schroeder & Gefenas, 2009, pp. 113-121; Kottow, 2004). The vulnerability has its origin in the physical and psychological helplessness of human beings towards themselves, their fellow human beings, their environment and their surroundings (see Ong-Vang-Cung, 2010, p. 119) as well as in their dependence on the world. A human being is dependent on him or herself, his or her fellow human, the context and the environment insofar as he or she can be injured by them and also be protected from injury by them (see also Butler, 2004, p. 77). Here, an essential difference becomes apparent between the understanding of "vulnerability" and the term "humiliation" (see Margalit, 1998). "Humiliation" refers only to human acts or omissions and not to the natural environment (see Margalit, 1998, pp. 9-10). However, the environment (understood as both the human and natural environment) is here also meant in its second sense, namely, as a source of vulnerability for human beings, because it can touch essential elements and spheres of human existence and because human beings have different ways of dealing with it and responding to it. Thus, people who have become victims of a natural disaster should not simply be left to their own devices but should receive support.

One can distinguish between two types of vulnerability The second type can be divided into three derivations:

- *Basic vulnerability (A)*, which is part of all humans and cannot be influenced by humans (e.g. human transience);
- *Selective and variable vulnerability (B)*,
  - which can be attributed to injustice;
  - which can be attributed to accidents;
  - which can be attributed to one's own fault.

All types of vulnerability may encompass different areas or aspects of human existence. On the one hand, there is physical or psychological vulnerability. Physical and psychological vulnerability belong to the individual and can therefore be referred to as *"internal areas and aspects of vulnerability" (C)*. The vulnerability turns to injuries in case of torture, violence, etc. Both physical and psychological vulnerability are not limited by human heterogeneity. E.g., people with disabilities are subjectively and objectively exposed to the same degree of vulnerability as people without disabilities.

The "inner areas and aspects of vulnerability" are to be distinguished from the *"external domains and aspects of vulnerability" (D)*, such as faith, religiousness, and worldview (see Barnes 2002, p. 3), law, food, medical care, education, financial benefits, infrastructure, etc. The vulnerability turns into injuries, deprivations, discrimination, and exclusion when disregarded (see Ferrarese, 2009). In contrast to the "internal domains and aspects of vulnerability" (C), the transformation of vulnerability into injury in the "external domains and aspects of vulnerability" (D) takes place outside the person. Of course, this does not mean that this transformation has no impact on the person or his or her inner spheres – on the contrary.

The *external form* (E) (possibility of attack and injury from outside) introduced above must be distinguished from the internal and external areas and aspects of vulnerability (possible attacks and injury from outside) and the internal form (F) (inability and lack of means for corresponding protection) of vulnerability), which can also occur in both types of vulnerability.

As for the second type of selective and variable vulnerability and its subtypes there is an interest in measuring and operationalizing the various disciplinary positions in order to respond to vulnerability with appropriate measures (see Alwang et al., 2002).

Humans share vulnerability with other living beings, which accounts for the moral relevance of the latter (see Ladwig, 2007). If one's own decisions and actions will cause pain to another living being it is morally relevant. Because if morality strives for the good life and right acts then the pain of another living being is important from two perspectives: one perspective is the perspective of the morally capable person(s). Morally capable means that the person is able to reflect self-determinedly on the good life and right action, to define moral rules, and to judge and act according to them. The other perspective represents the view of the morally needy being or the being with moral patience. Moral neediness is here not understood in the Kantian sense that it is a peculiarity of human beings that they need to moralize (see Ladwig, 2007). Moral need or moral patience means here that the objects of decisions and actions of an ethical character (e.g., animals), which are made or carried out by the morally capable depend on the ethical quality of these decisions and actions; i.e., they require a legitimacy that shapes the decisions and actions of the morally capable. Conversely, these objects are not morally indifferent to the decisions and actions of morally capable people. They make a difference when morally capable people strive for the good life and the right action, which in the example of animals is justified by their vulnerability. Moral need or moral patience does not depend on moral capability. To show moral relevance one can start from the standpoint of both the morally needy and the morally capable. For example, from the point of view of the morally needy or morally patient, it is morally wrong for someone to hit it. At the same time, from the point of view of the morally capable, it is morally wrong to hit a morally needy or morally patient person, i.e. to inflict pain on him or her (bad conscience). With vulnerability it is possible to rethink the relationship between moral need (or moral patience) and moral capability and to show the moral relevance of moral need or moral patience as well as moral ability.

One can approach the fact of shared vulnerability between humans and animals in another way, namely by noting that there is some evidence for the assumption – which will only be briefly touched upon here, as it is not central to the discussion of vulnerability in the context of ethical decision-making – that humans formulate animal welfare laws because of the vulnerability of animals. The immediate conclusion that humans and animals should have the same rights because they are both vulnerable is invalid insofar as three points (and the third point in particular) must be considered: *First,* humans – because of their vulnerability – agree on rights that apply to themselves as human beings. Moreover, humans also draft appropriate animal welfare laws for other living beings, such as animals, with whom they share vulnerability. These are based on their perception of themselves and their perception of their own vulnerability and, separately, on their perception of animals and their vulnerability.

Second, it is conceivable that people imagine or perceive that the vulnerability of humans and the vulnerability of animals are phenomenologically different. This connection does not imply an attempt to claim that this is actually the case empirically, neither in the distinction between human self-perception and the different perception of animals, nor in the finding of differences in the course of phenomenological consideration of the vulnerability of humans and animals. This is irrelevant to this approach. Rather, it is likely that humans – aware of and recognizing the vulnerability of animals – think of themselves as human beings that are different from animals, or that humans understand their own vulnerability which they share with other humans and which is different from the vulnerability of animals.

Third, the subsequent awareness of one's own vulnerability which opens up to the "first-person perspective" (see Runggaldier, 2003) and "self-relation" and is integrated into the principle of vulnerability, distinguishes the human being from other living beings. The principle of vulnerability is not only about the purely empirically perceptible vulnerability but above all about how the human being perceives and thinks about his own vulnerability. The focus is on the investigation and reflection of vulnerability and the moral consequences that the principle of vulnerability elicits in human beings. Vulnerability can mean, for example, that a person who is healthy today knows that he or she could become ill tomorrow. Or – while living happily today – that tomorrow he or she could be killed by someone. In this thought process the person goes through a process of uncertainty. For he or she becomes aware of their own vulnerability and ultimately their transience (see Hoffmaster, 2006, p. 42). This possibility of self-awareness applies to all people.

Becoming aware of one's own vulnerability is a process of self-awareness of a human being. The empirical correctness of it is not relevant. During this process when a person becomes aware of his or her own vulnerability he or she recognizes *ex negativo* the "first-person perspective" (see Runggaldier, 2003). This encompasses people's awareness that, as singular persons, they are subjects of self-awareness through which they access their own vulnerability. On the other hand, they experience this basic anthropological situation of vulnerability as a subject (i.e. in the first person singular). The actions, decisions, sufferings, and lives of people emanate from them as subjects. Furthermore, they interpret this basic anthropological situation of vulnerability as a subject: "For acting and suffering, he experiences himself as the living being who does not simply live like all other living beings, but who lives only by leading *his life*. To relate to himself, to act neither naturally nor arbitrarily, but to orientate himself to reasons and to pursue freely chosen purposes, constitutes the form of life that connects him with all human beings as *his equals*. At the same time, it makes him vulnerable, since the self-relation belonging to his form of life is dependent on fundamental conditions of realization" (Honnefelder, 2012, pp. 171-172, emphasis in original). The human being is able to enter into a "self-relation" with himself.

Since people are aware of their vulnerability but at the same time do not know if and when this vulnerability will manifest itself and turns into a concrete violation or transgression, they are willing to grant all people the "first-person perspective" and the "self-relation" based on the equality of all people, because this is the most rational, prudent and advantageous solution for them. Which means granting rights – human rights – to all people in order to protect themselves and all others, because vulnerability also includes the "first-person perspective" and the "self-relation".

Human beings are therefore not bearers of human rights because they are vulnerable, but because of the principle of vulnerability which leads to the enjoyment of human rights for all human beings. This differentiates them from the vulnerability of animals and serves as a *differentia specifica,* which allows a different understanding of the vulnerability of humans and the vulnerability of animals. The fact that vulnerability affects humans and animals therefore does not contradict the relevance of the principle of vulnerability for the justification of human rights.

Vulnerability, the "first-person perspective" and "self-relation": the principle of vulnerability probably covers what "consciousness,“ "free will,“ "self-reflexivity" (Misselhorn, 2018, p. 214), and "subjectivity" (Ohly, 2019, pp. 49-72) provide as distinguishing features between humans and machines or so called "artificial intelligence". At the same time, vulnerability, the "first-person perspective" and "self-relation" in their argumentative impact on the distinction between humans and machines (or so called "artificial intelligence") go beyond these distinguishing features because, *first,* they do not depend on the condition of an assumed dualism between mind (or soul) and body and therefore allow us to avoid this controversial issue. *Second,* and more importantly, they do not create a potential for discrimination. Making "consciousness", "free will", "self-reflexivity", and "subjectivity" *the* characteristics or capabilities among the many human characteristics or capabilities that distinguish humans from machines and so called "artificial intelligence", one runs the risk of discriminating against those humans who differ in these characteristics or abilities, such as people with disabilities, coma patients, or embryos. The risk of discrimination remains even when potentially held accountable. Martha C. Nussbaum shows this potential for discrimination clearly when – following this line of reasoning – she goes so far as to deny people with disabilities their humanity because they lack certain abilities, but still grants them moral relevance in order to weaken her argument: "[...] that certain severely handicapped infants are never human beings, even when born of two human parents: again, those with a global and total sensory incapacity and/or without consciousness or thought; also, I think, those incapable of recognizing or relating to others at all. (This, of course, says nothing about what we owe them morally; it only separates this question from moral questions about human beings.)" (Nussbaum, 1995, p. 82)

The absence of the principle of vulnerability is a first argument against the moral capability of machines and so called "artificial intelligence". The absence of vulnerability is an argument against considering machines and so called "artificial intelligence" as morally needy or as beings with moral patience. It could be argued however that the status of moral neediness or moral patience should be assigned to so called "artificial intelligence" by humans depending on their relationships with machines (see Coeckelbergh, 2012). The implicit arbitrariness that contradicts this view does not meet the requirements of critical rational ethics. Moreover, it could also be argued that it is ethically better to treat a morally valuable being better than its status deserves, rather than treating it as a mere object (see LaBossiere, 2017). This argument is limited however because this would presuppose that machines and so called "artificial intelligence" are beings and more than objects. Neither has been demonstrated so far (see Gunkel, 2018). On the contrary, the lack of vulnerability and identity (see DiGiovanna, 2017) outlined above contradicts the notion that machines and so called "artificial intelligence" are beings, and provides an argument for perceiving them as objects. This perception as objects does not automatically mean that humans have no ethical obligations towards them (see Bryson, 2010), because mistreating an object would change the human subject in an ethically negative way (see Kant, 1990), and because it does not preclude objects from having moral relevance insofar as their material value must be considered from the perspective of sustainability, including economic, environmental, and social dimensions.

4.3 Conscience

A second challenge to the moral capability of machines is based on the concept of conscience (see Kirchschlaeger, 2017d), which is of great importance for humans and their morality. The conscience combines what is objectively commanded and what is subjectively required in a specific and concrete situation, in a specific context or experienced in a unique encounter with unique people. "The conscience is an active faculty that discovers and recognizes the good in the complexity of any situation" (Hogan, 2004, pp. 86-87). The conscience creates an authority in a person which affects an action *a priori*, but also *a posteriori*. The conscience is a process that precedes an action, but also refers to critical questioning and examination after an action (see also Holzhey, 1975, p. 7; Schueller, 1980, pp. 40-57). But the conscience does not act of itself (see also Wolbert, 2008, p. 170). "Conscience does not assert itself when it suits one. Conscience asserts itself, often when it does not suit us at all. What conscience is, is not available to us in the end. [...] This experience does not stop. From this we learn that conscience is in the process of becoming, represents a process that is at once given and given up to us" (Mieth, 1992, p. 225). Conscience thus opens up the difference between the level of being and the level of ought (see Reiter, 1991, p. 11).

As a testimony to human moral capability the conscience connects people across cultures, traditions, religions, and worldviews. Conscience can therefore be located on a constitutive level of being human. It comprises the potential to recognize what is morally right and good and to classify it in the specific context of each case (see context (see Schuster & Kerber, 1996, p. 144).

Furthermore, the conscience describes an interaction between the normative system on which it is based and the inner aspects of the individual (see Kranich-Stroetz, 2008, p. 124). The former is also expressed by placing the individual in a social context with the resulting duties and the corresponding responsibility (see on the discourse on concrete questions of conscience Schaupp, 2014; Hoefling, 2014; Martinsen, 2004). The latter guarantees a critical distance of the individual from the normative system of a society (see Reiter, 1991, p. 15).

The relation to the self, the relation to normativity and the relation to a normative system are thus based on conscience or are united in it (see Kranich-Stroetz, 2008, p. 125). On closer examination, conscience can be understood as the "ability of the human mind to recognize moral values, commandments, and laws *(synderesis)*, but in a narrower sense their application to one's own actions to be carried out directly." (Schuster & Kerber, 1996, p. 144, emphasis in original; see on the philosophical discourse on the "conscience" Huebsch, 1995) The conscience assumes the role of an inner voice of human beings in moral questions and decisions. This inner voice is not always unambiguous, but the conscience struggles with itself and its decisions as the definition of Immanuel Kant shows: "The consciousness of an inner court in man ('before which his thoughts sue or excuse each other') is the conscience." (Kant, 1997, p. 572) Instead of a heteronomous understanding of conscience, in which conscience is determined by something that is alien to human freedom and reason, Kant uses autonomy to preserve the independence of the moral phenomenon or duty. Morality in the strict sense means that it is purely subject-related. Morality is the duty which a human being recognizes as something that his practical reason dictates to him as his duty. Not only acting in accordance with duty, but acting out of a sense of duty is morally good and morally right, because we can act purely dutiful for various reasons that have nothing to do with morality or even immorality. Since the conscience measures itself only by itself, a false conscience is impossible according to Kant. Acting according to one's conscience cannot be an additional duty, otherwise there would be a need for a conscience above the conscience. It is also up to the conscience itself to recognize what is a duty. The duty to form a conscience arises from the conscience itself. Only then it becomes a moral duty. In any other case, the duty would come from outside, would be externally determined and therefore not moral, but legalistic.

Practical reason is, so to speak, the antithesis of conscience. It reminds us whether an action is dutiful or not and determines the objects that are dutiful. It is deprived of all functions determined by content. Instead, the conscience is the duty in itself. Not conscience but practical reason decides on the content of the duty. Conscience judges only the relationship of humans to their duty like "an inner court of justice in man ('before which his thoughts sue or excuse each other')" (Kant, 1997, p. 572). Based on the autonomy of morality the conscience can be equated with a self-obligation of a human being.

The distinction introduced by Thomas Aquinas between the "primordial conscience" (synteresis) – the natural habitus in which the human being participates in the eternal truth of practical reason, which also contains the supreme principle of moral conscience "Thou shalt do good and refrain from evil" – as the basis of action, and the concrete conscience based on it or functional conscience, which consists in its application to concrete action (conscientia), is also helpful. (Thomas Aquinas, Summa theologiae 1 q 79 a 12-13; see Anzenbacher, 2015; Noichl, 1993, pp. 264-274). "Conscience helps, in the shaping of freedom to be realistic and reasonable – indeed, to recognize its moral limits and dependencies. But at the same time, it always gives courage not to resign and to believe in the possibility that one can actually change one's life according to moral convictions and ideals." (Roemelt, 2011, p. 58).

Building on this, the distinction of conscience into a "primal conscience," a "value conscience", and a "situational conscience" goes even further (see Teichtweiter, 1976). While the "primal conscience" focuses on the fundamental requirement to prefer good over evil and to act accordingly, the "situational conscience" decides based on the concrete situation which concrete actions of moral value should be taken while taking into account personal needs, natural inclinations, personal values, duties, and responsibilities. The "value conscience" mediates between the "primal conscience" and the "situational conscience" by taking into account personal impressions and attitudes. Thus, the mediation of conscience involves the various dimensions of morality which can also manifest themselves in the maturation of conscience. Based on this, the following can be said about conscience: "In its execution as a judgment, it is, like moral judgment, a manifoldly conditioned event, namely, one that is graded several times and whose content is determined by a great variety of variables. In the claim, on the other hand, which it holds habitually and brings to bear in judgment, it is completely unconditional, for nothing else is expressed in it in the mode of self-reference than that which is the ground of moral obligation in general, namely the selfhood of man as a being of reason and freedom." (Honnefelder, 1993, p. 121)

Conscience thus connects morality or duty with the various levels of a human being and his or her existence. The latter are of different quality and intensity and are shaped by individual development or social influences (see Schmitt, 2008). A human being also forms his or her counterpart. "Every claim of conscience draws on and replicates self-affirmation. Just as the self of affirmation is nothing solitary, so too conscience acts not silent, incapable of generalization, selfishly. [...] If conscience, in referring back to self-affirmation, repeats the decisive moment of the initiation of individuation and socialization, then in doing so it does nothing for 'solitary' and 'naked' self-discovery, self-selection, and self-realization." (Marten, 1975, p. 124)

Beyond that, conscience is about decisions, actions and omissions of a human in a single life situation that cannot be overlooked. All these situations lay claim to morality. A human being considers this claim in the most diverse ways. The object of moral action is shaping one's own life history. In the respective conscious decisions emotional moments are also included. Because "only reason [can be] the faculty that (in the act of conscience) relates the multiplicity of actions to an ultimate unity, namely to the success of human existence as a whole." (Honnefelder, 1982, pp. 32-33; see Honnefelder, 1993) This comprehensive concern also allows for many ways of knowing and perceiving conscience. "Conscience only fails to become an authoritarian controlling authority when it opens up, acts contextually, and builds its social-practical sensitivity and judgment from its own-critically accompanied view of reality." (Schmitt, 2008, p. 162)

At the same time, the individual is urged to examine the objective and subjective conditions by becoming aware of his or her own identity, self-understanding and self-assessment in conscience by reflecting on norms. Thus, the shaping and setting of norms becomes conscious. The conscience thus places itself at the service of the realization of the will in humans, so that it may come as close as possible to the first.

Furthermore, the horizon of conscience has an impact that does not end with a single decision or action, but encompasses the entire existence of the human being. Conscience proves to be "the patient path of learning freedom." (Roemelt, 2011, pp. 58-61)

The moral reasoning of a human being experienced in conscience and his moral ability to distinguish between good and evil makes conscience an absolute challenge for humans – again and again, when planning and considering an action in a final practical judgment that leads to action, and when, after an action, critically examining the questioning of this judgment with regard to its position on moral reason, its contribution to the success of being human, and its relationship to his or her own principles of action.

Finally, the conscience expresses a trust in the individual human being. The individual is expected to have this inner voice in moral matters, to recognize it, to listen to it, and then to act responsibly. It is respected and upheld that the dignity of conscience belongs to the individual.

Although, in the spirit of epistemic modesty, it must be pointed out that the determination of conscience is extremely complex and it must be remembered that one is attempting to make conceivable and plausible statements about the future on the basis of the present state of research. The following can nevertheless be stated: One cannot say that technologies have a conscience. The possibilities that technologies possess with regard to ethical decisions and actions do not even come close to those of the human conscience. They lack various levels of morality or duty and an existence anchored in conscience of varying quality and intensity which is shaped by individual development or societal influence (see Schmitt, 2008). Therefore, it cannot be said that technologies have a conscience. If one considers conscience as essential for morality the absence of conscience is a second argument against the morality of technologies.

It is not the strongest argument, because in the current discourse the conscience is coming under pressure from psychological and sociological as well as neuroscientific perspectives. In the former, they leave it at depth psychology approaches that still uphold autonomy but impose some limitations on it. The latter invokes evidence of neuronal processes and chemical-biological processes that only allow autonomy to be only feigned and conscience, in empirical truth, is nothing but the result of these processes (see Roth, 2003). These two lines of argument for questioning conscience can be countered with an analogy to Immanuel Kant's arguments concerning the mental freedom of man (see also Nida-Ruemelin, 2005): If this were true, i.e. if human beings were limited in their autonomy and were nothing but chemical and biological processes, how could it be explained that human beings can decide against "sensual stimuli" and act accordingly, or that humans are guided by "causes of motion which are imagined only by reason" (Kant, 1995a, p. 675)? Or that people often do what they do not want to do, but should do?

4.4 Freedom

A third question mark regarding the moral capability of machines arises from freedom. Freedom is a *conditio sine qua non for* morality because only freedom gives the possibility to decide for or against the good or the right. Freedom is ambiguous. As a formal relation, freedom can be described as "freedom from..." and "freedom to...". Freedom means to act according to one's own wishes and plans. At the same time, there is also a social horizon of freedom when freedom and human dignity of all people come into focus.

Furthermore, freedom is at the origin of science, research and technology. This aspect must be emphasized at a time when some voices deny the existence of freedom altogether. (see Holderegger et al., 2007; Fink & Rosenzweig, 2006; Fleischer, 2012; Bloch, 2011; Bauer, 2007; Achtner, 2010; Guckes, 2003) "Freedom, which is now denied, has made possible the developments of science in the name of which it is now denied. Indeed, science would never have existed without the human mind's inherent ability to distinguish between false and true and to prefer the true to the false. False and true make no sense if not for a free mind capable of striving for one and rejecting the other. Without this essential condition, any explanation remains merely a noisy, meaningless act. For this reason, it can be rightly said that science is the most glorious monument that freedom has erected to itself, and that scientific research is utterly inconceivable without freedom." (Hersch, 1992, pp. 60-61)

Machines have no freedom. Technologies are designed, developed and built by humans, which means they are produced heteronomously. Therefore, also the learning of ethical principles and norms is guided by humans. In the final analysis, machines would always be controlled from the outside. Figuratively speaking: machines – even self-learning machines – will go back to a first line of code, which always comes from humans. Freedom is a third argument against the moral capability of machines.

4.5 Responsibility

The freedom to want what one does not want is what characterizes responsibility. (see Kirchschlaeger, 2014a) Responsibility succeeds in combining one's own freedom with the freedom of all other people and respecting the human dignity of all people. Responsibility enables freedom to discover the horizon beyond one's own needs and interests for the freedom of all other people and for social tasks and goals. "Responsibility breaks down the individualistic freedom that is focused on one's own needs and integrates it into social structures, into common tasks and goals." (Holderegger, 2006, p. 401) Responsibility also forms a *conditio sine qua non for* morality.

Responsibility characterizes the awareness that one has to "give an answer" to someone, which leads to the concept of responsibility. One gives an authority – e.g. other people, in the case of legal responsibility the court, for a religious person God, a divine, a transcendent – a response in relation to one's own decisions and actions. The principle of responsibility is based on the necessity of providing these authorities with information about one's own actions, of giving an account and of being responsible for one's own decisions and actions. In order to be able to be a subject of responsibility, it needs freedom and rationality.

The question arises as to whether machines can assume responsibility. The answer must be negative because machines cannot be a subject of responsibility because they lack freedom – a fourth argument against the moral capability of machines.

4.6 Autonomy

A fifth fundamental question concerning the attribution of moral capability to machines arises from the autonomy proclaimed by humans for themselves. Immanuel Kant links the dignity of human beings to their autonomy (see Kant, 1974, p. 69). A human being is a bearer of dignity and must therefore not be instrumentalized, because as a rational being he or she recognizes general moral rules and principles for him- or herself, determines them for him- or herself, bases his or her actions on them and is the bearer of dignity (see Kant, 1974, p. 74). The dignity of man "as a rational being who obeys no other laws than those he has given himself" (Kant, 1974, p. 67) is based on a human's ability to set rules of reason for himself. This means that moral rules and principles which humans formulate in their autonomy, must meet the following requirements of a critical, rational morality, which guarantees their universality: universality implies the fulfillment of the principle of generalizability through the presentation of rational and plausible arguments – "good reasons". "Good reasons" means that it must be conceivable that all human beings, in their effective freedom and autonomy as well as in their full equality would agree to these reasons – within a model of thought and not within a real global referendum – on ethical grounds (see Kirchschlaeger, 2021a).

Does the description of human autonomy, which can be expressed by humans, corresponds to the potential of technologies (see, e.g., Decker, 2019a; Decker, 2019b; Thimm & Baechle, 2018) to follow moral rules, to take moral decisions and to perform corresponding actions? Regarding the notion of "autonomy" there is a gap between technology and ethics (see Kirchschlaeger, 2017c). While humans recognize general moral rules and principles for themselves, establish them for themselves and align their actions with them, technologies cannot do this. Technologies are primarily made for their efficiency and can establish rules as a self-learning system, for example to increase their efficiency. But these rules do not contain any ethical quality. Machines fail because of the above-mentioned principle of generalizability. This negation is a fifth argument against the notion of "moral technologies". This negation is further strengthened by the fact that technologies cannot have autonomy without freedom.[4]

What about "self-learning systems" and their moral capability? Self-learning systems are machines that strive for requiring as little human input as possible to achieve a goal. "The difference is that machines can now think, albeit in a limited way. They solve problems, make decisions and – most importantly – they learn." (Metzler, 2016) If self-learning systems could improve without human input, they might be able to improve ethically, which could ultimately lead to their autonomy. But even "self-learning systems" would contradict their moral capability because of their lack of vulnerability, conscience, freedom, responsibility, and autonomy as shown above. (This would also apply to artificial general

4 This aspect was also mentioned in the statement of the European Group on Ethics of Science and New Technologies to the European Commission, see European Group on Ethics in Science and New Technologies to the European Commission 2018a.

intelligence.) Since their self-learning is based on practical errors, the possibility of such a moral learning process is doubtful because the principle to not cause harm to humans always comes first. (see Neuhaeuser, 2012)

Does this assessment change with regard to the moral capability of machines in the case of "superintelligence" (see Bostrom, 2014) or more adequately (see Kirchschlaeger, 2021a): "super-data-based systems (super-DS)"? Super-data-based systems (Super-DS) are systems that are generally more intelligent than humans. Since machines already massively outperform humans in various areas of intelligence (e.g., memory, handling large amounts of data, etc.), it is to be expected that there will come further areas of intelligence.

Three forms of "super-DS" can be distinguished: Super-DS in terms of speed (like human intelligence, but much faster) (see Bostrom, 2014, pp. 53-54), collective super-DS ("superior performance due to the aggregation of a large number of smaller intelligences") (Bostrom, 2014, p. 54), and qualitative super-DS (which significantly outperforms human intelligence at a speed at least as high as human intelligence) (see Bostrom, 2014, pp. 55-57).

The question of the moral capability of super-DS is proving to be extremely relevant. "The challenge posed by the prospect of superintelligence, and how we can best respond to it, may be the most important and daunting challenge humanity has ever faced. And – whether we succeed or not – it is probably the last challenge we will ever face." (Bostrom, 2014, p. vii) Among other issues, there is the ethical question of what happens to humans when self-learning super-DSs decide to set their own goals.

Based on the above we cannot say that a super-DS would have vulnerability, conscience, freedom, responsibility, or autonomy. Therefore, it would also not be possible to think it with a moral capability.

However, this technological potential creates the ethical opportunity for super-DSs to make ethically better decisions and perform ethically better than humans, even though they do both because they see the long-term benefits to themselves that result from ethical decisions and ethical behavior. Their behavior is thus ultimately based on pragmatic reasons. (This would, of course, strictly speaking, undermine the ethical nature of their decisions and put their behavior into question.) Nevertheless, super-DSs might have these ethically speaking positive effects

Just to prevent a possible misunderstanding, if the moral capability of machines would be negated: machines can be programmed or trained with ethical principles and rules to achieve ethically legitimate decisions and actions (see Wallace & Allen, 2009; Moor, 2009), even if they themselves cannot recognize and determine them, and even if they cannot determine the ethical quality of principles and rules due to a lack of moral capability. Likewise, technologies can support ethical decisions of people (see Kirchschlaeger, 2021b).

Introducing several levels of "autonomy" (or morality) could be a possible counter-argument against such a positional reference of the denial of an ethical decision-making ability of machines: "Autonomy in machines and robots should be used in a narrower sense than in humans (i.e., metaphorically). In particular, the autonomy of machines and robots cannot be defined in absolute terms, but only relative to the required goals and tasks. Of course, it may often be the case that the results of the operations of a machine/robot are not known in advance to the human designer and operator. However, this does not mean that the machine/robot is a (fully) autonomous and independent actor that decides for itself what to do. In fact, machines and robots can be considered as semi-autonomous agents, in which case we can have multiple levels of 'autonomy' [...] [respectively] several levels of 'morality'" (Tzafestas, 2016, p. 2). These levels include "operational morality" ("the moral meaning and responsibility rests entirely with the people involved in its development and use, far from complete moral agency. The computer and software scientists and engineers who design today's robots and software can usually predict all possible situations that the robot will face" (Tzafestas, 2016, p. 73)), "functional morality" ("the ability of the ethical robot to make moral judgments when deciding on a course of action without direct instructions from the top down. In this case, designers can no longer predict the robot's actions and their consequences" (Tzafestas, 2016, p. 73)) and "complete morality" ("a robot so intelligent that it chooses its actions fully autonomously and is thus fully responsible for them. In fact, moral decision making can be seen as a natural extension of technical safety for systems with more intelligence and autonomy." (Tzafestas, 2016, p. 73)) Even introducing levels of autonomy or morality cannot address the fundamental criticisms outlined above. It remains problematic to consider "morality" or "autonomy" for a technological system that is heteronomously programmed to follow heteronomously defined principles and rules and is not able to autonomously define them for itself, autonomously decide to follow them or not, and to be aware of their ethical quality. It remains problematic to define "morality" or "autonomy" for a technological system that lacks vulnerability, conscience, freedom, responsibility, and moral capability.

A possible counterargument could be to refer to the stages of human moral development – e.g., in Kohlberg's model (see Kohlberg, 1981; Kohlberg, 1984) – and to claim that they are similar to these stages, and to derive why, if even humans at lower stages of moral development are considered "moral", this should not apply to the stages of "morality" of robots. This challenge could be met by pointing out that humans can seize the potential to develop their moral capacities (which may or may not be realized) as a basis for the appropriateness of understanding humans at lower stages of moral development as "moral".

While the definition of these levels as levels of "autonomy" and "morality" without linking them to "autonomy" and "morality" and without understanding them as "autonomous" and "moral" has been criticized, the distinction between these levels can be helpful in categorizing the different levels of the ability of technical systems to follow legal and ethical principles and rules, and, in the case of the last level, in distinguishing what is important for a system's autonomy and morality and rules to follow, and – in the case of the last level – in distinguishing what is appropriate for technical systems because of their lack of "autonomy" and moral capability.

4.7 Ethical Decisions of Humans

The above reflection leads to the main consequence that human beings are responsible for making ethical choices (see Johnson, 2006a; Yampolski, 2013).

This could provoke the criticism that this negation of the ethical decision-making capability of machines remains too firmly trapped in the dichotomy "man – machine". "Humans and technical artifacts are so closely intertwined in our everyday lives that even our moral perceptions and decisions are technologically mediated. Only when we acknowledge this interconnectedness of humans and technologies can we take responsibility for the ways in which technologies impact society and the human condition – in the practices of technology design, implementation, and use." (Verbeek, 2014, p. 76) Understanding artifacts as "moral influencers" (Moor, 2006, p. 18) or as "moral factors" highlights the positive or negative contribution of an artifact to realizing an ethical principle in an action or an outcome (see Brey, 2014). While it is true that people and technologies are interconnected, it must *first* be questioned whether invoking "contribution" does not lead to the conclusion that any material object can contribute to a positive or negative action or outcome vis-à-vis an ethical principle. For example, a stone can negatively affect the act of hitting someone by increasing the violence of that act and it can negatively affect the result of the hitting because the victim of that violent act can be seriously injured. Thus, since anything can be a moral factor, it cannot be said that this applies only to artifacts. Furthermore, the question arises whether the term "moral factor" has any epistemological meaning at all.

Secondly, loosening the dichotomy "man – machine" cannot go any further because the "demand for the preservation of the unity of the subject against the threatening danger of its functional splitting [exists]. It is important to see that this demand must not itself be misunderstood as moral. It is – and we cannot go back behind this 'paradigm' of Kant's moral philosophy – the condition of the possibility of ethics." (Mathwig, 2000, p. 288) There remains a fundamental difference between humans and technologies in terms of ethical subjectivity and moral agency, because having an effect or influence – which is true, because technologies can have an impact on human life, including on the ethical dimension – is not equivalent to possessing ethical subjectivity, moral agency, and ethical decision-making capacity. For example, the weather may have an influence on a person's mood, but no one would claim that the weather has moral agency with respect to a person's mood. As just explained, there are some preconditions for ethical subjectivity and moral agency that technologies lack. Therefore, technologies – although closely interwoven with humans – do not have ethical subjectivity or moral capability. Therefore, they cannot be attributed with ethical decision-making ability. The distinction between the "causal efficacy of artifacts in producing events and states", "acting for or on behalf of another entity", and "moral agency" (see Johnson & Noorman, 2014) reinforces this position, especially since it is not conceptually necessary to group all three under "agency", while the first two differ in their agency. Finally, if we look more closely at the interdependence between people and technologies themselves, an even more intense form of interdependence will not lead to dissolving the difference between the two. For example, if two people are in love with each other, as deeply as possible, and therefore experience the most intense entanglement imaginable, one would still not argue that the two individuals dissolve into one.

One way to overcome this problem and still push technologies toward ethical subjectivity and moral action is to change the understanding of morality. "We cannot find 'morality' in objects nor in autonomous subjects. It occurs only in the relations between subjects and objects, where objects have moral significance and subjects enter into mediated relations with the world." (Verbeek, 2014, p. 87) This would mean, for example, being able to blame the weather for people's moods, even though moods can be any way regardless of the weather. In other words, and this is a first counterargument against this adaptation of the understanding of morality, there is also a morality without technologies. Second, even if technologies can be ethically significant as objects, the ability to recognize what is ethically legitimate, to decide and act accordingly does not belong to them, but to the human being as ethical subject and moral agent, due to the above-mentioned lack of vulnerability, conscience, freedom, responsibility, and autonomy. *Third,* although technologies as objects "can perform morally relevant actions independently of the humans who created them and can bring about 'artificial good' and 'artificial evil'" (Floridi, 2014, p. 187), this is not a reason for extending the concept of moral agency to the point where technologies fit into this concept (see Floridi, 2014; see Torrance, 2008; Torrance, 2011). Technologies can bring about good and evil, but they do so without recognizing, knowing, or being aware of the ethical quality of those actions. It is true that "a computer can represent emotions without having emotions itself, and computer systems may be able to pretend to understand the meaning of symbols without actually having what would be called human understanding." (Wallach & Allen, 2009, p. 9) In both cases, representation and functioning lack authenticity, which is considered essential for emotions and moral capacities. In other words, for the accomplishment of its task a representation of emotion depends on representation being emotional, and functioning depends on having moral capability for the accomplishment of its task. In both cases, emotionality and moral capability would be negated for machines.

Fourth, only a human being possesses vulnerability, conscience, freedom, responsibility, autonomy, and moral capability. Therefore, one should avoid seeing "everything that exists – including oneself – from the point of view of the technically feasible. For example, many are ready to see themselves as highly perfected robots – or else, according to the scientific view initially chosen, as the result of biologically inherited characteristics. Such a view of the self has a profound impact on the 'I'. Those who see themselves in this way tend to reduce the 'I' to a sum of 'effects' whose 'causes' can be analyzed so that the claim to freedom and to their unbendingness in responsibility can be corroded at the root." (Hersch, 1992, p. 60)

Fifth, it is also the content of ethical decision-making by human beings and exclusively up to human beings to program technologies with ethical values, principles, and norms and/or train them to respect them – even if the technologies do not recognize their ethical quality. This leads to the question of what ethical values, principles, and norms should be taught to technologies (see Bhargava & Kim, 2017) – a topic that has been discussed elsewhere (see Kirchschlaeger, 2021a).

Sixth, the exclusive capability of human beings to recognize what is ethically legitimate, to decide and act accordingly also includes the possibility that an ethical decision-making process may lead to avoid creating, designing, producing, distributing, or using technologies as objects, or the possibility of choosing to abolish or destroy technologies.

This distinction between people and technologies makes it obvious who is entrusted with ethical decision-making and who is solely responsible for it: humans.

5 The Rule-Transcending Uniqueness of the Concrete

Summary

This chapter is dedicated to the characteristics of ethical decision-making that, on the one hand, it cannot rely on democratic opinion-forming and decision-making processes for its justification. On the other hand, it is characterized by a sensitivity for the *rule-transcending uniqueness of the concrete.* What is meant by this is that ethical decision-making goes beyond blind adherence to ethical principles and norms in that it has to strive for what is ethically right in each concrete situation in a concrete encounter with concrete people.

5.1 Ethics Is not Democracy

In their ethical decision-making processes, people have to consider something that is also true for ethics committees, for example (see Bobbert & Scherzinger, 2019; Duewell & Neumann, 2005, pp. 225-274; Huriet, 2009), and remains a fundamental conceptual challenge: ethics as a science is not democratic. A democratic process does not *per se* guarantee legitimacy. It is possible that a democratic opinion-forming and decision-making process may also lead to results that are ethically bad or wrong. Ethics must rationally and critically satisfy the principle of generalizability by presenting rational and plausible arguments – "good reasons". "Good reasons" means that it must be conceivable that all human beings, in their actual freedom and autonomy as well as in their full equality would agree to these reasons – zu within a model of thought and not within a real worldwide referendum – on ethical grounds (see Kirchschlaeger, 2021a).

5.2 Ethics Beyond Principles and Norms

Furthermore, people have to master the fact that ethics is not only about principles, standards, and rules. In order to cope with the complexity of ethics, its sensitivity for the *rule-transcending uniqueness of the concrete* (see Kirchschlaeger, 2021a) must be taken into account. This is, among other things, the reason why ethics is not casuistry. The following example can illustrate the complexity of ethics: Let us imagine a situation in the Nazi era in which we are hiding a Jewish family from the Nazis in our home. Suddenly, the Nazis knock on the door and ask us if we give shelter to a Jewish family in our home. If we follow the commandment to tell the truth, we send the Jewish family to a certain death. If we want to save the lives of the Jewish family we must lie to the Nazis. Now, what is the ethically right thing to do in this concrete situation, in this concrete encounter, with these concrete people? In this case, saving the lives of the Jewish family would have to be weighted higher than the commandment to tell the truth and, consequently, the ethically right thing to do would be to lie to the Nazis. Ethics and ethical decisions are characterized by their sensitivity for the *rule-transcending uniqueness of the concrete.*

The virtue of *epikeia* and the conscience play an essential role here. Epikeia involves the "rectification of the law where it is incomplete as a result of its general wording" (Aristotle, 1983, p. V, 14, 1137b, 26). *Epikeia* is an "independent practical judgment that evaluates the moral demands of a concrete situation in the light of moral principles and moral norms." (Schockenhoff, 2014a, p. 601) *Epikeia* consists of the "search for the greater justice" (Schloegl-Flierl, 2016, p. 29), it has to "stimulate and sustain the search for meaningful justice" (Schloegl-Flierl, 2016, pp. 29-30). *Epikeia* takes into account the fact that in a concrete encounter with concrete people in a concrete situation, rules reach their limits because the concrete in its uniqueness overrides the rule. "The generally applicable concrete ethical, the positive-legal and the many other norms are an indispensable prerequisite, but they are not sufficient to guarantee that basic stock of humanity which, in the face of diversity, saves this society from being torn apart and from the dire consequences that result from it. Inevitably, in the concrete situation, we must sometimes transgress norms in order to act humanely, without denying the need for norms or denying that they apply in general." (Virt, 2007, pp. 42-43) What is crucial here is, *first,* that this is not done to enrich oneself or to pursue a self-interest, preference, desire, or lust, but to achieve a higher ethical good in this concrete situation, in this concrete encounter, with these concrete people. *Second,* ethical and legal norms and their validity are of course not put into question by *epikeia. Epikeia* "guides not only the application of norms but also identifies the most pressing ones." (Keenan, 2010, p. 155) They are, *third,* made more effective by this justice striving for virtue. *Fourth, epikeia* at the same time ensures that the ethical and legal norms serve human beings and not the other way around (see Schloegl-Flierl, 2016, p. 39). "With the help of epikeia it is possible to act in a way that is appropriate to the situation and serves the human being." (*Schloegl-Flierl,* 2016, p. 39) *Fifth,* this also does not imply putting into question the meaningfulness and raison d'être of ethical norms in the sense of a call for anarchy.

Epikeia, however, requires ethically critical and constructive participation (see Demmer, 2010, pp. 110-113), "which presupposes the human being as a responsible person capable of creatively considering and interpreting norms and laws." (Schloegl-Flierl, 2016, p. 39)

Due to the increasing complexity of everyday reality, people are challenged to find insights into reality-adequate norms and to take them into account in a more differentiated and better way. In this context, human beings are expected to take responsibility for the shaping of norms. This responsibility aims at the fact that these rules must be critically questioned again and again and adapted for a perspective and ethical improvement of people.

This prospective, creative level also includes a human responsibility to create norms. "The perception of the moral claim does not at all mean merely a reading of normatively determined factual and meaningful behavior, but is always already a creative seeing and discovering. This seeing and discovering is creative in that the human being is called upon to risk new meaningful moments of the shaping of life in his imagination, which did not occur in the previous system of rules. The moral goodness of the person urges him to further develop what is humanly right in the form of models." (Virt, 2007, p. 43)

6 SAMBA

Summary

This chapter is dedicated to Ethics-SAMBA: Ethical decision-making challenges us every day – be it in our private or professional lives, be it on an organizational or institutional level, be it in a political or economic context. SAMBA encourages ethical decision-making with ease and argumentative elegance by the following four steps:

1. See and Understand the Reality
2. Analyze the Reality from a Moral Standpoint
3. Be the Ethical Judge!
4. Act Accordingly!

In the following, attention will be given to such a model on the basis of what has been established so far and within the lines already drawn. The SAMBA model aims to provide a concrete guide to ethical decision-making with ease and argumentative elegance to be effective in four steps. This model is intended as a concrete and practical framework for structuring ethical arguments, ethical discussions and ethical decision-making for ethics-students, students of all scientific disciplines, people in their professional as well as private ethical decision-making processes as well as decision-makers in politics, business and society. SAMBA is intended to show why decisions are made and how, and to enable people to make concrete ethical decisions and to act accordingly in an ethically sound manner.

SAMBA is composed of the following four steps:

1. See and Understand the Reality
2. Analyze the Reality from a Moral Standpoint
3. Be the Ethical Judge!
4. Act Accordingly!

For each of the four steps, tangible and achievable goals provide orientation. In addition, a number of guiding questions are provided to facilitate the practical and goal-oriented implementation of each of the four steps.

6.1 See and Understand the Reality

GUIDING QUESTION:

A. *What is your own horizon of knowledge, understanding, thought, language, and belief?*

GOAL:

The goal is to become aware of one's own horizon of knowledge, understanding, thinking, language, and belief/worldview, as well as assumptions based on these or connected with them.

In the course of an ethical decision-making process, as introduced above, it is important to strive for a critical distance – be it to reality or to morality – in order to make an ethical decision as objectively as possible. The first step in the right direction is to take a look at one's own horizon of knowledge, understanding, thinking, language, and belief/worldview, as well as the assumptions based on them or connected with them, and to deal with them self-critically. This horizon of knowledge, understanding, thinking, language, and belief/worldview could be the current state of research (knowledge horizon), current hermeneutics (understanding horizon), current limits of human reason (thought horizon), current language with its word creations, formulations, sentence constructions, forms of expression, and images (language horizon) and an attachment to and/or anchoring in a religion, faith, or worldview community or the consciously chosen opposite, namely a consciously chosen distancing from one or any religion, faith, or worldview community (faith/worldview horizon). "Although good ethical decision-making requires us to carefully take into account as much relevant information as is available to us, we have good reason to think that we commonly fall well short of this standard – either by overlooking relevant facts completely or by underestimating their significance. The mental models we employ can contribute to this problem. As we have explained, mental models frame our experiences in ways that both aid and hinder our perceptions. They enable us to focus selectively on ethically relevant matters. By their very nature, they provide incomplete perspectives, resulting in bounded awareness and bounded ethicality. Insofar as our mental modeling practices result in unwarranted partiality, or even ethical blindness, the desired reflective process is distorted. This distortion is aggravated by the fact that our mental models can have this distorting effect without our consciously realizing it. Thus, although we cannot do without mental models, they leave us all vulnerable to blindness and, insofar as we are unaware of this, self-deception." (Pritchard et al., 2013, p. 125)

GUIDING QUESTION:

B. *What is the current reality?*

GOAL:

The aim is to describe reality as objectively and neutrally as possible. For this purpose, studies from other thematically appropriate and adequate scientific disciplines can also be consulted. Part of this definition and delineation of reality are also the applicable legal regulations and standards that also constitute reality.

This description of reality should not be based on subjective and personal impressions, but (empirical) studies from other sciences that can competently contribute something to arrive at a perception of reality that is as objective and neutral as possible. Thus, for example, jurisprudential explanations of the legal situation, sociological analyses of social aspects or psychological studies with regard to human behavior and experience would have to be consulted. It goes without saying that this does not imply the expectation of becoming an "expert" in these different fields of science, but rather of forming an adequate picture of reality on the basis of the core statements from the relevant sciences.

One's own horizon of knowledge, understanding, thinking, language, and belief/worldview shapes the perception of reality, so that a dialogue with reality begins. It is a *dialogue* because one's own horizon of knowledge, understanding, thinking, language, and belief/worldview influences the perception of reality and the perception of reality can change the horizon of knowledge, understanding, thinking, language, and belief/worldview.

6.2 Analyze the Reality from a Moral Standpoint

GUIDING QUESTION:
A. *Where do you suspect an ethical question/challenge/problem?*

GOAL:
The goal is to determine the suspected ethical issue/challenge/problem.

For the time being, it is only an assumption, since the precise identification of an ethical question/challenge/problem is itself already oriented towards and based on an ethical reference point. (E.g. one recognizes global poverty in its ethical relevance as global injustice with the help of the principle of justice, which however (please see below in this section) has to be introduced and (please see below in this section) – rationally justified and reviewed for plausibility). However, this ethical reference point(s) must first be identified and then ethically justified, in order to then – and only then – be able to precisely determine the ethical question/the ethical challenge/the ethical problem.

This step, too, is to be classified as a dialogue event in the above sense, because the subject making an ethical decision is influenced by reality, and the ethical penetration of reality is shaped by the subject and his or her horizon of knowledge, understanding, thinking, language, and belief/worldview in the course of a mutual interaction.

GUIDING QUESTION:
B. *Is there really an ethical question/challenge/problem?*

GOAL:
The aim is to verify again and make sure whether it is really an *ethical* question/ *ethical* challenge/*ethical* problem, or a question/challenge/problem of a different nature (e.g. practical, pragmatic, economic).

While a practical problem requires a practical solution, a pragmatic problem needs a pragmatic solution "for something" that serves "someone", and an economic solution requires an economic answer that serves a rational and wise pursuit of self-interest, the ethical question turns out to be oriented towards an answer that is "in itself" right or good or wrong or bad, i.e. unconditionally and unconditionally ethically convincing. It needs to be verified whether it really is an *ethical* question/an *ethical* challenge/an *ethical* problem.

Furthermore, especially in view of the above-described dialogue process as a mutual interaction between the subject making the ethical decision and his or her horizon of knowledge, understanding, thought, language, and faith/worldview, it is important that the ethical decision-making process and the subject making the ethical decision and his or her horizon of knowledge, understanding, thinking, language, and belief/worldview examine the ethical penetration of reality again in the course of an ethical decision-making process in order to ensure that the ethical question/the ethical challenge/the ethical problem also arises in reality. This is adressing the risk that one may interpret something into reality that one does not find there. In the course of a renewed examination of the ethical quality of the question/the challenge/the problem as well as its relation to reality, it needs to be ensured that there really is an *ethical* question/an *ethical* challenge/an *ethical* problem which has to be addressed.

GUIDING QUESTION:

C. *Which ethical principles/norms/theories/approaches could provide orientation?*

GOAL:

The aim is to gain an overview of the plurality of ethics and which ethical principles (e.g. human dignity)/norms (e.g. human rights)/theories (e.g. virtue ethics, duty ethics, consequentialism (e.g. utilitarianism) or discourse ethics)/approaches (e.g. principle of responsibility with its eight dimensions; omni-dynamic social justice) can provide ethical orientation for this ethical question/challenge/problem.

When searching for ethical points of orientation for ethical decision-making it can be helpful to refer back to the goal of ethics. The goal of ethics is to "prove freedom as the unconditional in human want and action." (Pieper, 2017, p. 153) This requires to "critically examine every action performed or planned in principle to see whether it satisfies the claim of morality, i.e., freedom as an unconditional principle or whether it affirms unfreedom as the desired. Practice in moral freedom means practicing the critical distinction between good and evil, acquiring the ability of moral judgment, which only arises in the everyday coping with the respective existing situation, but which is made transparent by ethics in its meaning and function for human practice. [...] *Moral competence* is documented in the ability to act in all situations that require action, with regard to the principle of freedom to decide bindingly, i.e. with good reasons, what is to be done. Moral competence – as the modern concept of virtue so to speak – implies social responsibility in so far as the ability to act and judge morally, which is demanded of everyone, includes the readiness to respect the freedom of every human counterpart and to be accountable at all times for one's own actions before this freedom." (Pieper, 2017, p. 154, emphasis in original)

These considerations also discourage us from rashly seeing luck as a supposed criterion in the selection of the evaluation yardstick. "Happiness is not a normative but a descriptive concept of ethics. Humans should not strive for happiness since they always strive for it by nature. Rather, they should strive to always and everywhere act well and to the best of their ability, which is ultimately their happiness from a moral point of view." (Pieper, 2017, p. 141) Ethical orientation with regard to the selection of ethical principles, norms, theories, and approaches cause the good or the right. “Good and evil, in their original (moral) meaning are qualities of a will that determines itself (to freedom or to unfreedom). [...] An action is *right* if it achieves its goal; it is *wrong* if it fails to do so. A morally good action is not necessarily also right (*help comes too late or is completely insufficient*), just as a morally bad action is not necessarily wrong (*giving someone with a heart condition an overdose of digitalis is a successful way to kill them*). Or, to put it the other way around, not every right action is necessarily also good (*someone rescues a child who has fallen into the water, but not for the child's sake, but because he knows that it is the only child of a millionaire from whom he expects a high reward*), and not every wrong action is necessarily also bad (*someone goes to the lost and found office to turn in a valuable object he has found; since the office is already closed, he initially keeps it and eventually forgets to return it*). An action is ethically perfect if it is both (morally) good and (pragmatically) right. But whether an action is actually perfect is extremely difficult to decide empirically, since the good will does not express itself directly, but can only be inferred through the action. Thus, one can be wrong not only with respect to other people's actions, but also with respect to one's own actions” (Pieper, 2017, p. 150f, emphasis in original).

The selection of ethical principles, standards, norms, theories, and approaches is fundamentally shaped by the highest good. “The concept of the highest good unites the three great themes of ethics: bliss, freedom, and the good. The highest good is the horizon of meaning, within which human freedom finds its fulfillment by becoming the active consummation of a life practice that is happy as a whole.” (Pieper, 2017, p. 152)

Before we now set out to discover possible ethical reference points, it should be noted that the following brief reflections on options for ethical reference points must remain one-dimensional. Therefore the critical consideration of these options can never fully do justice to the individual approach due to the brevity of the respective explanations. The intention to extract essential aspects and to systematize these approaches to be able to appreciate them critically, is additionally aggravating in this respect. Finally, only a few possibilities can be picked out of an impressive abundance and variety of approaches, which cannot lead to a final judgment. At the same time, it should be noted that this abundance and variety of projects naturally serve the cause of ethics. For, first, they essentially strive to strengthen ethics which, despite possible weaknesses or gaps in an approach in a particular context or in a particular situation, they may nevertheless succeed in. Second, regardless of their persuasive power, they each expose specific aspects of ethics.

In the following, ethical principles which could serve the ethical decision-making are discussed and justified. “Principle, Latin principium, is a translation of the Greek arche and means 'origin' and 'beginning', but also 'rule' (see Latin princeps, ruler). Philosophically, the meaning of principium is primarily ‘the origin’ [...]. Alternatively, one finds also 'first cause' or 'first beginning' to clarify the difference to a purely temporal beginning or accidental beginning (lat. initium). [...] All uses of 'principle' have in common that principles provide reasons, but as principles they cannot be justified in the same way as what they are capable of justifying. Their validity is unconditional; they cannot be traced back to anything else." (Herrmann-Sinar, 2010, pp. 2143-2144) Because of their claim to universality as part of ethics they must fulfill the principle of generalizability by presenting rational and plausible arguments – "good reasons". "Good reasons" means that it must be conceivable that all human beings, in their effective freedom and autonomy as well as in their full equality would agree to these reasons – within a model of thought and not within a real global referendum – on ethical grounds (see Kirchschlaeger, 2021a).

Ethical decision-making in the sense of *normative ethics* – meaning within the framework of an ethics which, in contrast to *metaethics* (critical theory of ethics that analyzes the structure of ethical reflection) and in contrast to *descriptive ethics* (empirical description of moral ideas and convictions, which therefore does not judge normatively) strives for generally valid, argumentative justifications for what is morally good and right as well as for moral obligations and it makes ethical evaluations, can be *virtue-ethical* or *norm-ethical:*

- *virtue ethics* evaluates character traits and attitudes from a first-person perspective - and thus a participant perspective as humanly good or bad (see Marschuetz, 2014, pp. 145-156),
- *normethics* judges concrete actions as humanly right or wrong from a third-person perspective, which means from an observer perspective (see Marschuetz, 2014, pp. 175-179).

Both unfoldings of ethics – virtue ethics and norm ethics – will be discussed in the following as guidelines for ethical decision-making.

Virtue Ethics

Virtues prove to be "attitudes or [...] ways of being that are assumed to be good for both the individual and the community. [...] The virtues are at the same time moral recommendations for the individual and ultimately his happiness and well-being as well as enabling the common good." (Fellsches, 2010, p. 2781ff)

Virtue ethics approaches contribute significantly to ethical decision-making with epikeia introduced as virtue in chapter 5 The Rule-Transcending Uniqueness of the Concrete.

Virtue ethics approaches reach their limits when it comes to ethical decision-making, since ethical decision-making must do justice to ethical plurality. "A central difficulty consists in answering the question of how happiness can be defined more precisely today as the supreme good which is pursued for its own sake. How can one still speak today of a supreme good to which all aspire, and how can a generally shared substantive concretization of the formal principle of happiness still be possible? Insofar as views of happiness always refer to a respective self-understanding of human beings, there is the problem that such self-understandings can no longer be formulated in a consensual way within an anthropology" (Marschuetz, 2014, p. 163).

Normethics

Normethical approaches that are open to ethical decision-making include, among others:

Authoritative Approaches

One option for ethical orientation is the authoritative way. In this case, authorities such as persons, texts, traditions, sciences, etc. serve through experts as orientation for ethical decisions. An authoritative approach to ethical decisions follows the argumentation pattern "person XYZ said that ...", "in text ABC it says, ..." (see Marschuetz, 2014, pp. 179-199).

An authoritative approach to ethical decision-making knows the risk of a missing rational justification. Even if there is a rational justification if, for example, an authority figure strives for a rational justification it does not take effect if the argument is only authoritative and not rational. "The only problem is that, as a rule, humans only accept justifications whose claim to validity can be recognized and acknowledged by the person concerned. They thus demand rational arguments that are comprehensible to them and others" (Marschuetz, 2014, p. 181).

Natural Law

The natural law approach assumes an order given to humans, which exists independently of humans and exists by itself. This order applies everywhere equally and in this sense is universal (see Marschuetz, 2014, pp. 199-215). "Natural law has the same force of validity everywhere and is independent of consent or non-consent (of people)" (Aristotle, 1983, p. 1134). Natural law is based on a variety of understandings of "nature". Natural law as an ethical instrument reaches its limits in the course of ethical decision-making

- as it lacks rational justification, because it would not guarantee the criterion of fulfilling the principle of generalizability;
- involves the danger of a naturalistic fallacy. This means that normative statements of ought are derived directly from empirical observations without asking whether what can be observed empirically would also be valid ethically;
- remains trapped in a circular argumentation. The latter means "that something is derived from nature that was *previously* projected into it" (Marschuetz, 2014, p. 211, emphasis in original).

Discourse Ethics

Discourse ethics opens the horizon that, against the background of a plurality of ethics, ethical decisions should be guided by what people would be able to agree on in the course of an intersubjective process of understanding (see Marschuetz, 2014, pp. 215-223). Thus, discourse ethics according to Juergen Habermas is based on the moral principle: "According to discourse ethics, a norm may only be valid if all those potentially affected by it as participants in a practical discourse reach an agreement that this norm is valid" (Habermas, 1983, p. 76).

In addition, there is the principle of universalization, which must be observed in the course of a discours eethics approach: "Thus, every valid norm must satisfy the condition that the consequences and side-effects which in each case result from its *general* observance for the satisfaction of the interests of *each* individual (presumably) can be accepted (and are preferred to the effects of the known alternative possibilities of regulation) by *all* those affected" (Habermas, 1983, p. 75ff, emphasis in original).

Discourse ethics is characterized on the one hand by its high plausibility and methodological clarity.

On the other hand, the pragmatic question arises whether such a consensus is even possible and achievable.

Furthermore, it is important to note that a compromise is not necessarily ethically legitimate.

Finally – and probably most importantly – it should be borne in mind that a discourse ethics approach carries the risk of discriminating against people who cannot participate in a discourse (e.g., people with severe intellectual disabilities, etc.).

Teleology / Consequentialism

A teleological approach – the term derives from "telos" (in Greek the goal, the purpose) – orients itself in ethical decision-making on the evaluation (under consideration of a highest goal/purpose) of the expected effects or consequences. The latter also leads to calling this approach "consequentialism". What comes into play here is the consideration of the subject's responsibility for the consequences of his or her actions (see Marschuetz, 2014, pp. 223-232).

A teleological or consequentialist approach knows the risk of relativizing the morally good, since after all a "bad" action can lead to "good" consequences, in the sense of "the end justifies the means." This is also accompanied by the loss of the testimonial character of moral action, since an action that is actually morally bad but causes morally good consequences is ennobled as ethically right. Finally, a teleological or consequentialist approach struggles with the impossibility of adequately weighing the consequences.

Utilitarianism

Utilitarianism ("utilitas" means usefulness in Latin) relies in its evaluation in the service of ethical decisions on the principle of utility, having also its core in the weighing of the consequences (see Marschuetz, 2014, pp. 232-238). Utilitarianism is an empiricist conception, since only empirical experience forms the basis for determining the highest good. Under the principle of utility is to be understood "the principle that approves or disapproves of every action to the extent that it seems to have a tendency to increase or prevent the happiness of the group whose interest is in question." (Bentham, 1975, pp. 35-58). It characterizes utilitarianism that it is based on a hedonistic understanding of "happiness" as well as a hedonistic conception of humans and that there are no intrinsically morally right or wrong actions. Likewise, it is to be noted that with adjusting the luck of the group a social principle comes into play and thus no mention of an egoistic hedonism.

From a practical and pragmatic point of view, a utilitarian approach focusing on the principle of utility would fit well with the economic considerations and the pursuit of efficiency that currently dominates the social subsystem of the economy and from there spills over to other social subsystems as well as society as a whole. "The utilitarian principle means the principle that approves or disapproves of every action according to the tendency it seems to have to increase or decrease the happiness of those whose interests are in question: or, in other words, to promote or counteract this happiness" (Bentham, 2007, p. 1).

From an ethical point of view, the principle of utility can be opposed with the following counter-arguments, which weaken its ability to provide ethical guidance. It raises the question if the hedonistic concept of "happiness" can do justice to the task of steering ethical decision-making processes. (However, It must be acknowledged that this problem can be adapted to use "suffering and its absence" as a way to apply the concept of "utilitarianism" in this area, which is not the case for the following points). Moreover, since an utilitarian approach cannot serve *per se* as an ethical reference point for identifying ethically right or wrong, as part of a reality that need to be analyzed ethically, as has been discussed above. Moreover, anthropology, which is purely empirically accessible, proves to be too narrow to consider the effects of a decision on a person's self-understanding from an ethical perspective.

Furthermore, a utilitarian approach recognizes the limit that "happiness" is not always quantifiable because human existence is a far more complex reality.

Moreover, a utilitarian approach is unable to cope with the complexity of ethics outlined above: A utility is not always universally determinable.

Also, utilitarianism is not up to the task because it is not robust and comprehensive enough to determine what would mean a right action in these types of cases. In addition, utilitarianism's particular emphasis on quantification is misleading, since many important factors in the answer to the question, namely, "What is a right action in circumstance X?" are not quantifiable, or at least not easily quantifiable.

Furthermore, the application of a utilitarian approach to an ethical decision carries with it the risk of promoting the "happiness" of a majority at the expense of the "unhappiness" of a minority.

Finally – and this is probably the most important counter-argument – a utilitarian approach could stand for the irrelevance of the individual and disregard the human dignity of all human beings.

Deontology (Duty Ethics)

The term "deontology" comes from "to deon", which in Greek stands for the intended and the obligatory. The starting point of a deontological approach is that certain actions or types of actions are in themselves morally right or wrong and that moral absolutes exist. These bind people under all circumstances, even if results or consequences of the action are negative, less useful, or unwise (see Marschuetz, 2014, pp. 223-229). With regard to a deontological approach, however, it is important to note: "By no means *all*, but only certain actions are regarded as deontologically justifiable. Since such actions are compulsory regardless of their external consequences and circumstances, they must obviously serve for the protection of the highest moral values, which would be relativized or disregarded in their significance by consequential considerations or circumstantial exceptions. The absolute prohibition of torture, for example, seeks to protect the core content of human dignity, which must be respected at all costs. If this prohibition, according to the deontological argumentation, were not valid in itself, then exceptions to the prohibition of torture (e.g., with regard to certain consequences which one seeks to achieve through torture, or certain circumstances by means of which one seeks to justify it) would be always possible. But that would mean an ethically unacceptable disregard for human dignity." (Marschuetz, 2014, p. 225, emphasis in original)

A deontological approach knows the risks of rigorism, uncompromisingness, and the exclusion of consequences. These can be addressed in that a deontological approach also considers the consequences of an ethical decision. "It remains to be noted that deontological norms despite their unconditional claim to validity, have always been limited – namely with regard to unacceptable *consequences* which would be connected to an unconditional adherence to them. Such a limitation is only possible on the basis of *teleological* considerations. Even more: the answer to the question of what actions are to be justified deontologically and what are not, presupposes teleological points of view. The *aim of* a deontologically justified prohibition is always to avoid the consequences that such an act would cause. A deontological justification of norms is therefore not conceivable without consequence-oriented considerations. However, it is primarily concerned with the consequences that are *internal* to the action, i.e. those consequences that a certain action causes by itself. Secondarily, of course, consequences external to the action are also relevant, if certain consequences of this action are subsequently limited by exceptions. The often claimed opposition of deontological and teleological norm justification thus begins to waver" (Marschuetz, 2014, p. 228f, emphasis in original).

Rather, the deontological and the teleological approach are to be thought as interacting, even if they remain different approaches. "Basically, it should be noted that the deontological standard underlying a teleological argumentation is located exclusively on the level of principles, but not on the level of concrete norms. For this reason, a consequence-oriented judgment of action commits only in general (or prima facie) and not in itself. Therefore, it is not, or only to a certain extent, able to identify the moral claim, which can be experienced in conscience. Of course, this should not to be understood as always being a disadvantage. In innumerable areas of action, the teleological justification of norms represents procedure without alternative for the ethical evaluation of actions [...]. One needs to think here especially of fields of action which are not at all adequately accessible to a moral judgment without corresponding factual knowledge. [...] Deontological justifications for mandatorily binding prohibitions of action are therefore indicated where it is already recognizable at a first glance and also generally understandable that the morally good is fundamentally disregarded." (Marschuetz, 2014, p. 238f) Accordingly, "deontological justifications of norms show their indispensable strength when it comes to protecting human dignity in its core area" (Schockenhoff, 2014, p. 421).

The envisaged interaction between duties and consequences and an individual as well as a social perspective concretizes the ethical principles of "justice" since this also involves a balance between individual and collective interests, "responsibility" – here the acting subject in his or her freedom comes as *one of the principles of all principles of ethics* in relation to the consequences of his or her decisions into focus, since "responsibility" is not only retrospective but also prospective – and "human rights", to which the protection of human dignity and freedom as *the two principles of all principles of ethics* is entrusted.

The ethical principles "justice", "responsibility", and "human rights", which are proposed in the following for ethical evaluation are, of course, not the only ethical principles, that might be helpful in the search for ethical guidelines for ethical decision-making. They do not constitute an exhaustive list. These three ethical principles were selected,

1. because their normative validity can be ethically justified (see Kirchschlaeger, 2013b, 2014c, p. 54, 2016b);
2. because they are essentially relevant, or closely related, to the two *principles of all principles of ethics* freedom and human dignity;
3. because they are fundamental.

The Principle of Responsibility

What is "Responsibility"?

The term "responsibility" is not only frequently used in politics and business today, but is also central to the normative discourse (see Kirchschlaeger, 2014c). It is striking that responsibility in the political and economic discourse is used in the sense of "competence". *First,* "responsibility" implies a bearer of competence. *Second,* the term implies a precise definition of the object or situation for which someone is responsible. *Third,* the time frame of responsibility is clearly defined and limited. Looking at the use of the term "responsibility,“ the suspicion arises that it lacks at least three relevant elements of the concept of responsibility: the characteristic of care, the temporal definition of care as *ongoing care,* and the ethical obligation that is part of responsibility.

The term "responsibility" was originally used in the history of ideas (Grimm & Grimm, 1956, sp. 79-82) when someone explains or justifies a decision or justifies an action before a judge. This judgment may be earthly or heavenly. From this original place in life, which has a juridical character, it also becomes clear how the basis should to be classified from which "responsibility", that is to say "to give an answer", is derived and leads to the concept of responsibility. People answer to God and/or to the court for their decisions and actions. The concept of responsibility refers to the need to respond to these entities regarding one's own decisions and actions. The concept of responsibility thus proves to be a relational concept from the outset, because it can only be thought in terms of relationships – in this case, the relationship between a person who normatively assumes responsibility before a court or before God, and the court or God to whom he or she normatively responds (i.e., takes responsibility in the sense of accountability).

In the 18th century, the triumph of emancipation begins, which also has to do with responsibility. (see Schoenherr-Mann, 2010, p. 7f) In retrospect, it can also be seen that the use of this term gains intensity in the 19th century (see Heidbrink, 2003). One reason for this is that the term "responsibility" replaces the term "duty". This is due to the fact that "'duty' – if it is understood in a concrete, ethical-material sense and not as a moral commitment to morality (Kant) – [...] [is associated] with the idea of a clearly delineated scope of tasks and functions, of binding and unambiguous tasks (duties), which exist for one's own person (and its ultimate cause) or are given to one based on a certain position of a person within a group or society. This presupposes a more or less clear definition of the situation to which these duties can be easily applied. But the dynamism of the fields and the very often multi-layered problem areas can seldom be captured by the establishment of unambiguous, clearly defined duties but captured and described in terms of a clear area of responsibility" (Holderegger, 2006, p. 396). Responsibility is an open-ended and less tangible concept that corresponds to the "far more difficult social degree of complexity" (Korff & Wilhelms, 2001, p. 598) it is intended to do justice to. This complexity is composed of the messy causation of human decisions or actions and their consequences in industrial and post-industrial contexts, the anonymization of subjects and objects of decisions and actions, and the human decisions and actions, as well as the human recognition and general questioning of institutions based on people's limited self-awareness. "In the sign of technology, however, ethics has to deal with actions [...] that have an unprecedented causal reach into the future, accompanied by a prior knowledge that also goes beyond anything unique, as usual incomplete [...]. All this puts the responsibility into the center of ethics" (Jonas, 1985, p. 8f). On the one hand, the above-mentioned self-awareness leads to the fact that humans take it upon themselves to direct events despite the complex and confusing initial situation. This is expressed by the concept of responsibility. "A discussion of the future of humanity is about how the important basic features of the human condition can change or remain constant over time" (Bostrom, 2009, p. 186).

On the other hand, the term "responsibility" is intended to indicate that someone is responsible for the consequences of industrial and post-industrial contexts, which are manifested above all in the marks of massive human interference with nature and can no longer be regarded as the results of natural processes. This means, first of all, a narrowing of the concept by opening it up and expanding it to "competence,“ which means the management of "situations of action that are increasingly difficult to define and evaluate in advance, but nevertheless inevitably belong to the actors' sphere of competence" (Holderegger, 2006, p. 396). Even if it is demanding and remains a challenge to establish a causal connection between, for example, world hunger, poverty, environmental degradation, and climate destruction, someone is responsible for it and must take the blame.

Second, this also means that in the demarcation from natural events a bearer of responsibility emerges, who is a decisive and acting subject and who has freedom. For only with freedom can the subject of responsibility take responsibility for something. This connection goes back to Aristotle, who distinguishes between "voluntary" and "involuntary" and mentions voluntariness as a prerequisite for an action to be criticized (see Aristotle, 1983, p. 15).

At the same time, this also means that the subject of responsibility must be morally capable. Thus, it is only after 1850 that the use of the term "responsibility" was extended to include the concept of moral competence, which implies freedom and moral capability of the subject of responsibility. "Responsibility is a general need in the life of humans as moral beings, who act from insight and freedom and are bound by duty." (The Great Herder, 1935). The ideas of autonomy and the person contributed to this development. John Locke's understanding of the person as a subject of attribution (see Locke, 2006, p. 435f; Trotter Cockburn, 1702) and Immanuel Kant's definition of the person as "that subject whose acts are accountable" (Kant, 1997, p. 223) laid the foundation for an understanding that increasingly focused on the concept of responsibility. They also clarify the close connection between autonomy, person, and responsibility.

Finally, Jean-Paul Sartre underscores this close connection by acknowledging "that the human being, condemned to be free, must bear the burden of the whole world on his or her shoulders; in his or her being he or she is responsible for the world and for him- or herself" (Sartre, 1943, p. 696). For Sartre, responsibility means being at the center of "consciousness, the indisputable creator of an event or a thing" (Sartre, 1943, p. 696). According to Sartre, humans have to accept that they are the subject of responsibility.

If one looks at the development of the term "responsibility" from today's perspective, it becomes clear that certain elements of its current usage can be rediscovered. On a formal level, responsibility is about the relationship between a subject and an object, based on a standard before an authority.

The above-mentioned thoughts of Sartre are radicalized insofar as the human being in the above-introduced concept of responsibility, understood as competence, is often the subject of responsibility without simultaneously being the subject of action. While from the perspective of duty the human being is only bound by duty if the subject of duty is identical with the deciding and acting subject, responsibility in the sense of competence also allows someone to be a bearer of responsibility, regardless of whether he or she is also the deciding and acting subject. For example, a finance minister may turn out to be responsible for a financial crisis and must resign, even though he or she was most likely not the decisive and acting subject for the entire financial crisis in its complexity. Rather, in a so-called "risk society", which is characterized by a "multidimensionality of its causal relationships with inevitably ever new uncertainties to be managed" (Korff & Wilhelms, 2001, sp. 599) actual structural issues are assigned to individuals as responsibilities.

Modern secularization eventually led to the following changes in the understanding of responsibility: "God as the authority responsible is now and in the future replaced by the totality of all rational beings and possibly also by non-human nature... The scope of responsibility is extended, especially where humans are aware of a fundamental unpredictability of their consequences which is closely connected with a fundamental change of the subject of responsibility which obviously has to give up its limitation to the individual, as well as its limitation to those actions for which it was itself consciously responsible" (Zimmerli, 1993, p. 105).

Eight Dimensions of Responsibility

When responsibility is understood as accountability, there is a danger that responsibility is understood only and exclusively on an individual level and retrospectively and will only focus on the attribution of results and effects on someone. This risk must be overcome, on the one hand, with an understanding of responsibility which places the perspective in the foreground and ensures that decision-making- and action-competences are distributed in such a way that today's world and the environment today and in the future will not have to suffer from current action and inaction. (see Jonas, 1985)

On the other hand, in addition to individual responsibility the focus must also be on the responsibility for structural and institutional issues. For example, the social security gaps that lead to inequities must be addressed as a structural problem in a responsible manner. In addition, globalization, for example, remains the key to success for some countries in the world, but not for all. In the context of globalization, the emphasis has been on growth and wealth creation. But in practice and, surprisingly also in theory, the issue of distribution has been neglected (Enderle, 2002, p. 21). Some countries continue to be excluded from the positive effects of globalization, whether through their own fault (e.g., lack of political stability, corruption) or through unfair behavior by their globalization partners (e.g., protective tariffs, protectionism). While some countries have made great economic leaps in the years of increasing globalization, other countries are stagnating or falling behind because they are excluded from the global playing field or are only allowed to participate in economic and political competition under worse conditions. The consequences are poverty, war, and terrorism. This corresponds to Karl-Otto Apel's call for a "responsibility of humanity in solidarity of mankind" (Apel, 1988, p. 15).

Thomas Pogge, for example, calls for taking responsibility for institutional questions with regard to the enforcement of human rights. He calls for a focus on institutions and "*institutional systems and our global system of institutions, [...] with a view to assessing and reforming their relative contribution to the realization of human rights*" (Pogge, 1999, p. 379, emphasis in original). He starts his reflections by characterizing the relevant issues as institutional challenges, because "*the realization of human rights depends essentially on the structure of national and global basic orders, and these orders must be intelligently (re)structured for this purpose.*" (Pogge, 1999, p. 379, emphasis in original) Of course, individuals and governments in regions with human rights deficits are also responsible for institutional issues. However, Pogge rightly emphasizes that governments and citizens of richer countries bear even more responsibility for ensuring that the current world order, in which human rights are the rights of a minority, will be transformed into an order in which human rights are truly accessible to all. Referring to Article 28, Pogge rejects the position that human rights violations committed by people in other states have no direct normative impact on us (see Pogge, 1999, p. 394).

The approaches of a "collective responsibility" (see Wolf, 1993) and a "responsibility of the system" (see Buehl, 1998) go in a similar direction.

In a responsibility reflected in its ethical depth and especially in view of the continuous developments of the conceptual understanding of responsibility in terms of structure, institution, collective, and systems, the implicit relations of responsibility need to be clarified. It also needs a justification of who is the subject of responsibility and why, who or what means the object of responsibility and why, to what extent and why, in which way and why, in which intensity and why, before which instance and with which yardstick is this responsibility measured and why. Otherwise, there is a danger that the pressing challenges and problems and the responsibilities associated with them will be obscured by an open and intangible concept of responsibility. The rationale of who is the subject of responsibility and who or what is the object of responsibility, as well as before which instance and with which yardstick this responsibility is measured, is not simple. It "appears [...] extremely difficult to rationally justify an intersubjectively valid normative basis on which a basic responsible attitude demanded by authorities could be oriented towards and legitimized" (Holderegger, 2006, p. 395).

Before attempting to establish a purpose and a justification of the relationships contained in responsibility, one must attempt to define what "responsibility" means. Responsibility is a moral principle for decisions and actions which defines the relationship between a subject of a decision and a certain form of action (one-digit, two-digit, three-digit) of a person concerned or the results of a decision or action to a certain extent (sole or shared responsibility; intensity; scope of responsibility), in a particular manner (responsibility; accountability; liability; retroactive liability; prospective responsibility; care; or prevention) (see Bayertz,

2010, p. 2862; Holderegger, 2006, p. 398f) where it refers to a standard before a judging authority.

Based on the relationships contained in the responsibility it must be integrated into an eight-dimensional matrix: the dimension of the subject of responsibility, the dimension of the form of responsibility, the dimension of the object of responsibility, the dimension of the scope of responsibility, the dimension of the type of responsibility, the dimension of the volume of responsibility, the dimension of the scale of responsibility, and the dimension of the instance of responsibility. The various dimensions of responsibility can be defined and combined in different ways, so that, depending on the relationship character of the responsibility, it will result in different characteristics of the responsibility.

In the dimension of the *subject of responsibility,* individuals, collectives such as states, religious, cultural, traditional, or worldview-based communities, corporations, organizations, or institutions (i.e., "an organized collective") (see Bayertz, 2010, pp. 2861-2862) are subjects of responsibility. At a first glance, also "accidental or latent groups" could be perceived (see Bayertz, 2010, p. 2862) as subjects of responsibility. The fact that they have "no internal structure and no common goals and norms" (Bayertz, 2010, p. 2862) means that a relationship to other dimensions cannot be defined. Therefore, they cannot serve as subjects of responsibility because otherwise the aforementioned obfuscation of urgent need for action and pressing challenges is caused by unclear responsibilities. In the case of "incidental or latent groups" the subjects of responsibility within the group must be carefully traced back and determined to avoid such obfuscation.

The "responsibility orientation" (Holderegger, 2006, p. 400) arises from the subject of responsibility. The decisive filter for the definition of the dimension *subject of responsibility* is the fact that responsibility as explained above, presupposes freedom. Only living beings that are free can become subjects of responsibility. "Responsibility and freedom are corresponding concepts. Responsibility presupposes factual – not temporal – freedom just as freedom can only exist in responsibility. Responsibility is the freedom of humans given in the bond with God and neighbor alone." (Bonhoeffer, 1992, p. 283)

In addition to the basic function of freedom for responsibility and the resulting decisive effect on the determination of the *subject of responsibility*, responsibility also shapes freedom. "The freedom of humans is a 'relative' one and has to convey itself in view of the events given in what he or she does or does not do. The responsibility is then the instance that intervenes in the tension that exists between personal freedom and what is given and imposed." (Holderegger, 2006, p. 400) Responsibility, especially a "comprehensive, caring trait of responsibility" (Holderegger, 2006, p. 400) makes it possible for freedom to grow beyond self-reference into social reference. "Freedom thus gets a, precautionary' character, for one shows a willingness to deal creatively with tasks, mandates, obligations, etc., that have been given or transferred to one, or that one has acquired, with regard to the lives of others. The responsibility breaks the individualistic freedom that is focused on one's own needs and integrates it into social structures, into common tasks and goals." (Holderegger, 2006, p. 401)

This social embedding of freedom through responsibility is strengthened by the fact that, according to Julian Nida-Ruemelin and following Immanuel Kant, rationality also includes the triad of freedom, rationality, and responsibility (see Nida-Ruemelin, 2011, pp. 14-18). "*Rationality* expresses itself in a way of life that integrates the multiplicity of reasons in a coherent way. Insofar as we are guided by reasons, our form of life is not merely the result of processes that can be described in scientific terms; we possess a certain degree of *freedom*. Others consider us *responsible* for our form of life, our actions, judgments, and feelings, within the limits in which reasons are effective. Where reasons no longer play a role, where natural facts and laws determine our behavior, we are no longer considered responsible." (Nida-Ruemelin, 2011, p. 17, emphasis in original) On the one hand, rationality as a precondition of responsibility limits responsibility to the fact that in cases in which the supposed object of responsibility cannot decide freely and act, and in which reason is irrelevant, it does not enter into a relationship of responsibility with the supposed subject of responsibility. On the other hand, the requirement of reason demands responsibility and freedom in the way that responsibility not only as individual responsibility or freedom in its pure self-reference, but also as caring responsibility or freedom in its social reference.

Freedom and rationality and the triad freedom, rationality, and responsibility on the individual level can also be applied to other possible subjects mentioned above in the dimension of the subject of responsibility if, for example, special interests of institutions are taken into account.

This triad of freedom, rationality, and responsibility has a direct influence on the dimension of the subject of responsibility by shaping the definition of the dimension of the subject of responsibility. But it also has an influence on the other dimensions.

The dimension of the *form of responsibility* contains the number of digits with which responsibility can be understood, e.g., one-digit ("I am responsible"), two-digit ("I am responsible for my actions"), three-digit ("I am responsible for my actions towards you"), etc. With respect to the possibility of a one-digit form of responsibility one can agree with Julian Nida-Ruemelin "that the normative ought is unconditional in the sense that it is not an ought vis-à-vis a commanding or norm-giving authority, and that this normative ought is perfectly intelligible and deeply rooted in our lifeworld practice." (Nida-Ruemelin, 2011, p. 24)

The way how the dimension of "form of responsibility" is determined has a direct impact on all dimensions except the dimension "object of responsibility", since the object of responsibility must be determined to fit within the logical structure of the dimension "form of responsibility".

The dimension of the *object of responsibility* describes for whom or for what we are responsible. Individuals and the collectives mentioned above, "actions" (see Nida-Ruemelin, 2011, pp. 19-33), "beliefs" (see Nida-Ruemelin, 2011, pp.

33-47), "attitudes" (see Nida-Ruemelin, 2011, pp. 48-52), consequences, effects, and results of decisions and actions, as well as objects are to be located in the dimension "object of responsibility".

The interdependence of the responsibility dimensions underlying the matrix can be shown especially in the dimension of the *object of responsibility*. If, for example, one wishes to analyze the relationship between the dimension of the *object of responsibility* and the dimension of the *type of responsibility* (see below), then, in the case of a retrospective responsibility of consequences, the consequences, effects, and results of decisions and actions are the objects of responsibility. When considering a prospective care or prevention responsibility, individuals, collectives, and objects should be considered first and foremost. When determining more precisely for example the above-mentioned potential objects of responsibility – individuals, collectives, and objects – the dimension of the *volume of responsibility* has a decisive influence, because it defines, for example, the determination of the object of responsibility, whether one understands the volume of responsibility to be global, intergenerational or something else.

The dimension of the *scope of responsibility* determines in two respects how far responsibility extends, *first*, whether the subject of responsibility is able to share this responsibility with another subject of responsibility or bears it alone; *second*, whether the responsibility that the subject of responsibility bears is ethical, moral and legal, moral and political, or moral, legal and political, which determines the intensity of the responsibility.

The dimension of the *volume of responsibility* raises the question of whether the area of responsibility is defined as local, regional, international, global, current, or intergenerational.

The dimension of the *type of responsibility* can be seen in the sense of responsibility "for doing and not doing something in general, and in particular for tasks, roles, functions or offices that can be attributed to it" (Holderegger, 2006, p. 398). The latter can be understood in the context of "accountability" when "one is accountable to an authority (be it fellow human beings, courts of law, one's own conscience or God) [one] has to give account." (Holderegger, 2006, p. 399) Another type might be "liability", where "one is responsible for misconduct or neglect of responsibilities, tasks, duties etc. [and has] to answer for them" (Holderegger, 2006, p. 399).

Furthermore, it is possible to define the type of responsibility as a retrospective responsibility for results. This is based on clarifying the question of guilt in a particular situation.

Finally, the nature of responsibility can be seen as a prospective responsibility of care or prevention: The idea mentioned above of not limiting causal scope to things in the past, but also including the present and especially the future, and taking into account how decision-making and action are distributed, leads to a responsibility of care and prevention as a mode of responsibility to prevent the present world and the environment from struggling with the results of today's actions, now or in the future.

The dimension of the *scale of responsibility* is used to evaluate the consequences, effects, and results of decisions and actions, the conditions of persons, and the conditions of objects. "Causal attribution as such is normatively neutral; it acquires its moral dimension only through an act of evaluation" (Bayertz, 2010, p. 2862). This evaluation is based on the standard formulated by a system of values and norms.

The dimension of the *instance of responsibility* derives from the legal background of the term responsibility and shows that one has to answer to an authority. The instance of responsibility can be the conscience (see Kant, 1997, p. 438), the moral community, the people concerned, the divine, God, or the transcendent (see Bayertz, 2010, p. 2863).

After attempting to grasp the concept of "responsibility" the next step is to determine and justify the dimensions and relations of responsibility. Here, the emphasis is deliberately placed on a procedural rather than a material definition, since the former does more justice to the abundance of possible concretizations of the individual dimensions and relations. Moreover, in view of this abundance, it is necessary to start from a concept of responsibility with an identical core and not from different concepts of responsibility (see Nida-Ruemelin, 2011, p. 14).

The definition and justification of the dimensions and relations contained in the responsibility must meet the requirements of ethics, namely the fulfillment of the principle of generalizability by presenting rational and plausible arguments – "good reasons". "Good reasons" means that it must be conceivable that all people, in their effective freedom and autonomy as well as in their full equality, would agree to these reasons – within a model of thought and not within a real worldwide referendum – on ethical grounds. This means that the reasoning towards the subjects of responsibility and, if necessary, the objects of responsibility must be made in such a way that it is acceptable to the subjects and, if necessary, the objects of responsibility by taking into account the various dimensions of responsibility – especially the dimension of scale and the dimension of instance.

The term "meta-responsibility" (Bayertz, 1995, p. 60) makes it clear that humans are not only responsible for the consequences of their actions, but also for the consequences of their theories. It is hoped that with this contribution the consequences of these theoretical explanations do not remain theoretical.

Responsibility as a Principle for Ethical Decision-Making

The principle of responsibility serves ethical decision-making processes. On the one hand, it emphasizes the long-term horizon of ethical decisions of people: "If the new nature of our actions requires a new ethics of far-reaching responsibility which coincides with the scope of our power, then it also demands, in the name of this same responsibility ‚a new kind of humility – a humility not like the earlier humility, i.e., due to smallness, but due to the excessive size of our power, which is the excess of our power to act over our power to see and evaluate and judge our power" (Sandler, 2014, p. 45). On the other hand, it takes one's breath away because of "the critical vulnerability of nature to human's technological interventions that could not have been anticipated before it became evident in the damage that had already been done. This discovery [...] changes the concept of ourselves as causal agents in the overall scheme of things. It brings to light that the nature of human action *has* de facto changed and that an object of an entirely new order – no less than the entire biosphere of the planet – has been added to that for which we must be responsible by virtue of our power over it" (Jonas, 1985, p. 26f, emphasis in original). Finally, the principle of responsibility succeeds in crystallizing the need to make ethical decisions and to assume and bear responsibility accordingly.

The Principle of Justice

What is "Justice"?

Justice can be defined in different ways, e.g. Plato writes, "the having and doing of one's own and what belongs to oneself" (Plato, 1989, p. 434a). Ulpian thinks justice is the strong and constant will to give everyone his right ("iustitia"). ("*iustitia est constans et perpetua voluntas ius suum cuique tribuendi*") (Ulpian, 2005, pp. 1-10, emphasis in original). Another possibility is the demand to "treat the same equally in principle " (Honecker, 1990, p. 188) or, in other words, "an action is just if it gives everyone what is due to him or her" (Gosepath, 2010, p. 835). It has already become clear that justice is a "relational concept" (Gosepath, 2010, p. 835).

Another option goes even further and relates justice to morality in general: "If justice is to be considered a moral virtue it must be understood in a very broad sense that characterizes a person who does not unjustly violate any of the moral rules. In this sense, justice is, of course, not just one moral virtue among many, but rather the combination of all the moral virtues associated with moral rules." (Geert, 1970, p. 157) This includes that justice is necessary, but not sufficient, for the morally good (see Geert, 1970, p. 157). If one understands justice in the context of morality it becomes clear that one can distinguish between justice as "a measure of the external relations of persons and social structures [...]" and "[...] a virtue or inner attitude of humans" (Veith, 2004, p. 316).

"Inner" and "outer" justice build on the moral capability as a prerequisite for human decision-making and just action. Just actions and decisions are only possible if one can make them of one's own free will and is thus also responsible for them. Subjects of justice must therefore fulfill these prerequisites.

There can be different objects of justice: persons and their actions, decisions, institutions in a broader sense, analytical considerations, creative thoughts, outcomes of human interactions (e.g., contracts), biographies, distribution of goods, or political solutions (see Gosepath, 2010, p. 836).

Furthermore, justice according to Peter Koller can be divided into four concepts of justice (see Koller, 2005). This differentiation can provide an orientation for decisions and scope of action, which make it possible to be just and fair in each specific and individual situation:

1. Transactional Justice (e.g. equality of performance and consideration (e.g. wages)).
2. Political justice (democratic co-determination processes in which an impartial exercise of power serves to grant each individual his/her rights and social coexistence).
3. Corrective justice (compensatory damages to make up for harm and punishment to make up for wrongdoing).
4. Distributive justice (equal distribution of common goods (e.g. educational opportunities, access to the labor market, income opportunities) and burdens (e.g. taxes)).

Justice strives for equality or equal treatment. In the first concept of justice, equal things are treated equally and unequal things are treated unequally (see Aristotle, 1983, V, 6-7). In the second and third concepts of justice, all people are treated equally. In the fourth concept of justice, distributive justice, equality or equal treatment can be measured by the following three criteria: *merit, need,* or *equality.*

Equal treatment based on *merit* means that equal performance leads to equal consideration. In this way, inequalities (e.g. in wages, property, etc.) that arise due to unequal performance are justified.

Needs-based equality means that all people are entitled to the same level of need satisfaction. However, the individuality of people includes, among other things, different needs that require specific, unequal measures to achieve the same level of need satisfaction (e.g. special support measures, social security, etc.).

Equal treatment on the basis of *equality* means that goods and burdens are distributed equally among people (regardless of merit, need, etc.) to correspond as closely as possible to the equality of all people (e.g. access to education). Differences in terms of merit, need, etc. are neglected. Thus, all people have equal access to the same number of services without taking into account their differences. The equality of services corresponds to the differences of individuals: people are only equal if all people can satisfy their different needs to the same extent.

In other words, on the one hand, inequalities or unequal treatment based on *merit, need,* and *equality* are accepted under certain circumstances. On the other hand, it becomes obvious that, depending on the concept of justice, the moral evaluation of a decision, an action, or a status may differ. Finally, a decision or an action can be unjust even if its decision-making process is based on the free will of the consenting persons. All of this, among other things, accounts for the broadness of the concept of justice. At the same time, it is precisely at this point that there is a need for clarification.

The definition of the horizon of justice proves to be controversial. The duties that arise from justice can be understood with a universal or a particular dimension.

Linked to both problems is the question of the reference level of justice because this helps to clarify. What does one refer to when deciding which concept of justice to use and to what extent?

All four concepts of justice can be looked at from the point of view of "social justice" (see Kramer, 1992, p. 45). Social justice can be summarized as "giustizia fra uomo e uomo" (Taparelli, 1855, p. 354). "Social justice" is not an independent concept of justice, but influences one or more concepts of justice (see Giers, 1957; Anzenbacher, 1998, pp. 221-224). Social justice must be understood dynamically, with "programs and roles [to be] reformulated accordingly to meet the changing reality" (Glatzel, 2000, p. 148). Social justice aims above all to create a "just order, in which the most diverse interests of groups and individuals must be balanced and brought into the right relationship to each other" (Glatzel, 2000, p. 148). The meaning of social justice can even be extended "*as the moral consideration of such principally equal freedoms or the continued moral-practical effort to create the conditions of possibility under which freedom can be realized in social space as participation in all processes concerning it. But this realization must be supported by an ethos that gives form and stability to such realizations of freedom in structures and institutions.*" (Nothelle-Wildfeuer, 1999, p. 85, emphasis in original) A similar view is to see social justice as justice for the common good, which "spaces [open] for addressing the issue of problems of justice not only with regard to the state, but to various social actors. This becomes increasingly important where, for various reasons, the role of the state at any rate, if not of politics in general, is increasingly reduced and the responsibility for social acceptability or intolerability of the prevailing conditions is shifted accordingly more and more to institutions in civil society or in the private sector" (Hoppe, 2002, p. 37).

Apart from the decisions which, according to the above, require justification, the use of the term "justice" must be justified. If, for example, people and their actions, decisions, institutions in a broader sense, analytical considerations, creative thoughts, results of human interactions (e.g. contracts), biographies, distribution of goods, or political solutions are called just, it needs to be justified. In this challenge, we need to be guided by impartiality: if one takes an impartial standpoint, one will judge someone or something as just or unjust. In order to take this impartial standpoint, there are four models of thought in the current justice discourse (see Gosepath, 2010, p. 837): the accidental independent observer (see Smith, 2004), a role reversal of the participants (see Baier, 1974), universalizability (see Hare, 1992), or the "veil of ignorance" (see Rawls, 1971).

In addition, reasons must be given when a claim to justice is formulated, or if moral duties arise from a claim to justice. These can be, among other things, a reference to natural law, respect for human dignity, a right of justification, reciprocity of benefits for the parties involved, or an idealistic discourse (see Gosepath, 2010, p. 837).

The Tension Between Law and Justice

Justice can mean enacting societal laws to provide order. If there is no order yet or the state of a society does not correspond to justice, it is the task of justice to change this and to introduce a just order.

When there is order in a community or society, the rules and regulations that implement this order must be respected in the interest of *general justice*. Aristotle can be summarized as follows: Just is he who respects the laws. Since laws are based on a legislative act, this gives them their legitimacy (see Aristotle, 1983, V, 1-3). This means, for example, that the executive and the authorities of a state must implement the applicable laws precisely and professionally.

Nevertheless, solidary justice can emphasize the tension between law and justice. This can arise from the fact that the existing order of a community or society can never be as it should be. The pursuit of a pure and perfect expression of justice *in itself* requires constant corrections and adjustments to a changing reality. Laws formulated as expressions of legal reasoning may fail to achieve their goals, may be harmful to the community, or may be unlawful in a new, real-world context. In this situation, those who benefit from the situation will try to maintain that injustice as positive law is upheld. The disadvantaged will try to fight against this unjust treatment in order to get out of this situation. In this context, justice is not understood as a duty based on the affirmation of the law, but rather as *social justice*, which is directly related to the common good. Aristotle understands justice in this sense also as equality (see Aristotle, 1983, V, 1-2): Social justice (see Nothelle-Wildfeuer, 1999, pp. 86-343) requires, for example, the executive and the authorities of a state, but also civil society and the population to be aware of the decisions and actions of the government and the authorities, so that they use their decision-making and actions in such a way that they are just and fair in each of the concrete and individual situations. Too narrow and strict laws that leave no room for interpretation would lead to *unjust* situations in certain cases. Contextualization is necessary because it is neither the task of nor possible that legal regulations can precisely regulate all possible situations of human existence. The decision and scope of action is a challenge, because in the course of contextualization there is the danger of arbitrariness. Human rights can be used as a clearly defined ethical point of reference against arbitrariness. Ethics has a special significance in this critical evaluation, because it examines "whether the actually existing social systems, conditions and institutions, as prerequisites for a good life for all individuals, meet the criteria of justice and the common good." (Remele, 2009, p. 194) This critical task is possible because of a normative attitude toward laws and institutions that is open to change. This attitude is based on the perception of a complementary responsibility to obey norms, orders, and institutions, as well as a responsibility to shape them (see Remele, 2009, p. 194).

Omni-Dynamic Social Justice

Given the four concepts of justice presented above, transactional justice, political justice, corrective justice, and distributive justice and their respective difficulties or challenges, the question may arise how to deal with these four concepts of justice from an ethical perspective and which of the four concepts of justice are preferrable. The concept of *omni-dynamic social justice* addresses this question. Based on the above, it is not a question of excluding one or more concepts of justice, but rather of thinking about them from an ethical perspective, *first* in connection with the guiding principle of social justice, and then applying this to all four concepts of justice.

Second, these four concepts of justice must be thought together in order to avoid a one-sided approach to justice and to arrive at a comprehensive understanding of justice. All four concepts of justice are perceived in a *negative coherence* to each other. In contrast to the positive togetherness this does not mean that justice must always encompass all four concepts of justice. *Negative coherence* means that all four concepts of justice must be integrated or rational reasons must be given if one or more concepts of justice cannot be considered. Justice is thus understood as *omni-dynamic* (since it is thought in the interaction of all four concepts of justice).

Third, on the basis of what has been said so far, it makes sense from an ethical point of view to focus on distributive justice – on the one hand, in determining the relationship between distributive justice and the other concepts of justice, and on the other hand, in its practical implementation. In both cases, distributive justice is thought together with the guiding principle of social justice. In this sense, justice is to be understood as *omni-dynamic social justice.*

The primacy of distributive justice for the equality of all people can be justified by the human dignity of all humans and by the human rights of all humans, which are explained and ethically justified in the following subchapter.

The human dignity of all humans and human rights are also used as reference terms or *tertium comparationis* in the material definition of the *omni-dynamic social justice* and in the formulation of criteria as reference terms or *tertium comparationis*. For *omni-dynamic social justice* must be oriented towards something. For example in the case of distributive justice it must be defined, on the one hand, what is to be distributed justly and, on the other hand, what criteria can be used to ensure that the distribution of what is to be distributed is indeed just. When deciding on the material level of taxes, the following challenge arises: "Ideas of justice are pluralistic in that they cannot all be explained by a single fundamental principle of distribution; rather, when people are asked to judge the justice of a distribution of goods, people typically invoke several distributional criteria and arrive at an overall judgment by weighing these criteria against each other." (Miller, 1992, p. 558) In this context, ethics provides an orientation: "All modern concepts of justice accept a common basic norm: all human beings are to be respected as equal in principle, i.e., endowed with equal dignity. Therefore, every human being should be treated with equal respect and equal consideration. Depending on how the various concepts of justice understand the basic norm of equal dignity in more detail, different understandings of what is appropriate or just among equals arise in each case." (Gosepath, 2010, p. 837) There is a need for such a basic norm: "With regard to the common good as a target value, the following idea proves to be central: on the one hand, there is a widespread conviction in contemporary thought that, under the conditions of modernist thought and with a view to pluralistic and individualized societies, it is no longer possible to unfold a concept of the good or successful life filled with content, to which both the political community and the individual would be bound. On the other hand, the talk of the common good articulates the currently highly topical realization that human coexistence in society can only succeed if there is at least a minimal consensus with regard to certain indispensable foundations of the value-bound coexistence of the members of a society." (Nothelle-Wildfeuer, 2008, p. 148)

For example, distributive justice requires that human dignity be independent of, or even opposed to, human behavior in the establishment of justice and equality (see Wolbert, 2003, p. 167), that human dignity is not transformed into something realizable (see Wetz, 1998, p. 181), and that people's human dignity is not denied on the basis of particularly serious human rights violations committed by them.

Moreover, human dignity dominates the material determination of distributive justice insofar as it has to take into account the moral dimension of humans, "human's capacity for morality. As a person, we have a state of self in that we can relate to ourselvesand our actions, reflect on ourselves, and freely determine our own forms of life and basic attitudes." (Witschen, 2002, p. 14) On the other hand, it must not disregard the essential, non-moral elements of human existence (such as food, shelter, basic medical care, etc.) (see Witschen, 2002, p. 15).

An answer to the question of the horizon that distributive justice must encompass can be derived from human dignity. Through the consideration of human dignity it becomes clear that the human being must be in the center of the material determination of distributive justice. If distributive justice revolves around the human being (and not, for example, around special relationship, closeness, membership in a certain collective, origin from a certain territory, etc.), it must be universally conceived and refer to the global horizon. Against the background of human dignity a justification for a local horizon would have to put forward good (i.e., rationally justified) reasons of why distinctions can be made between people that justify a local horizon of distributive justice. For example, one might list, among other things, the differences in horizons of justice that result from comparing John Rawls's "A Theory of Justice" (see Rawls, 1971) with John Rawls's "Law of Peoples" (see Rawls, 1999) (see Singer, 2004, pp. 176-180): While in "A Theory of Justice" Rawls designs a system of justice with a balance between the affluent and the disadvantaged in a society with a local horizon for the common good, he rejects such a balance in "Law of Peoples." The latter implicitly involves a distinction between people that cannot be legitimized because it cannot be rationally justified. Thus, this distinction cannot be rationally convincing, because it would break with human dignity, since the latter manifests the equality of all people as human beings. "1 Any form of solidarization that is based on simultaneous disregard of the claim to universality of human dignity is ethically reprehensible.

[...] 2. every form of solidarization which meets the claim of human dignity only with regard to one's own group and its objectives, remains ethically deficient." (Korff, 1989, p. 45)

According to these considerations, justice consists in not only responsible relations between the individual and his/her fellow human beings, between the individual and society, but also between society and societies – with a universal horizon.

If, however, *omni-dynamic social justice* must be conceived with a global horizon, it follows, on the one hand, that the corresponding duties must be conceived on a *universal scale.* On the other hand, with regard to the material scope of the obligation, it must be considered that not "only" all humans are addressees of this obligation, but all humans *as* humans (i.e. people who are given the opportunity to live as humans with human dignity).

Finally, all three relationships – between the individual and his/her fellow human beings, between the individual and society, but also between society and societies – cannot be justifiably limited in time. This means that distributive justice must be thought of intergenerationally and with a universal horizon. Intergenerational justice essentially consists of four postulates: to consider future generations in all actions; not to consume more resources than will grow back; to distribute resources equitably on a global level; to respect natural rhythms (see Vogt, 2005, pp. 141-159).

Omni-Dynamic Social Justice and Intergenerational Justice

As an ethical tool for ethical decision-making, the principle of justice understood as *omni-dynamic social justice* should give more weight to the perspective of the future by considering future generations as subjects and objects of justice and the future as a horizon of justice. "Intergenerational justice" can be defined as follows: "A society is intergenerationally just when each generation contributes its fair share to ensuring that members of succeeding generations, within and beyond its borders, can meet their needs, avoid serious harm, and have the opportunity to enjoy things of value." (Thompson, 2010, p. 6; see also Vogt, 2005, pp. 141-159) "Intergenerational justice" frames the horizon of justice not only as global – in which all people are seen as potential subjects and objects of justice – but also as an "intergenerational continuum that extends indefinitely into the future" (Thompson, 2010, p. 6) and that opens up to the past in recognizing what previous generations have contributed and sacrificed (see Thompson, 2010, p. 6) and what injustices they have suffered. The boundaries of this intergenerational continuum remain open. This makes it more difficult to precisely understand what intergenerational justice means because, especially in the case of the future, one does not know exactly what to expect (see Wolf, 2003). "In our efforts to do justice to future generations, we move in a fog of uncertainty. Uncertainty does not mean that justice between generations is impossible or that it does not matter what we do. The response to uncertainty is to be as rational as possible –

to examine the available evidence and act accordingly – and to do the best we can to mitigate known risks." (Thompson, 2010, p. 9)

The concept of "intergenerational justice" seems to be an adequate principle to fairly balance the needs and interests not only of present people, but also of past and future generations. "Intergenerational justice" faces the challenge that the challenges and problems of the present are more pressing than those of the future, and that the indefinite temporal openness of "intergenerational" provokes a need for clarification and a distance between the present subjects and objects of justice and the future subjects and objects of justice. Moreover, the practical relevance of "intergenerational justice" must be demonstrated in the face of the highly complex and difficult-to-manage world of the present. The idea of being able to estimate future developments with the necessary precision in order to be able to define justice-relevant responsibilities, duties rights and claims, seems to be unattainable for human beings.

Moreover, the legitimacy of "intergenerational justice" must be ethically justified, in part because it is infinite and presumably a starting point for any desire. In the following subsection, this will be addressed in the justification of human rights based on the principle of vulnerability.

Answering the question of how we can justify intergenerational equity increases the burden of proof, because an assessment of justice in the present by constructing impartiality (or an impartial standpoint) within the discourse of the present moral community (e.g., using the "veil of ignorance") (see Rawls, 1971, pp. 136-142; Dierksmeier, 2006) can be justified, whereas intergenerational justice must also justify why the potential subjects and objects of intergenerational justice also include future generations of people (see Gosseries, 2008). In this question, human rights as an ethical reference point play an essential role, because one can approach the challenge of justifying intergenerational justice by pointing out that if it can be justified that all human beings (including future ones) are bearers of human rights, then their human rights must be respected in the present and in the future, and there is therefore an ethical need for intergenerational justice.

Also, the idea of intergenerational justice is fraught with doubts and skepticism as to whether it is realistic at all. "This line of reasoning rests on two assumptions: that people are predominantly self-interested and that their interests give them no reason to care about the fate of future generations or of people in other countries." (Thompson, 2010, p. 18) These assumptions can be challenged by "the uncertainty about what to do and how to do it, and the anxiety of those who believe they will be seriously disadvantaged" (Thompson, 2010, p. 19) as being the key challenges to achieving intergenerational justice which "stem from institutional failures rather than deficiencies in human nature" (Thompson, 2010, p. 19). Combining this observation with human rights as an ethical reference point, this institutional approach comes close to an institutional understanding of human rights: "According to the interactional understanding of human rights, governments and individuals have the responsibility of not violating human rights. According to my understanding of institutions, however, it is their responsibility to work for an institutional order and a public culture that guarantee safe access to the objects of their human rights for all members of society." (Pogge, 2002, p. 65) While the institutional understanding of human rights – and as a consequence of intergenerational justice – can be considered an important force for their realization – it seems difficult to demonstrate why institutions or systems of institutions or the global system of institutions (the totality of all institutions worldwide) should be on a different level than state and non-state actors, and why such human rights-related threats (or concerns of intergenerational justice) are only official threats, because they are not appropriate for the role of state and non-state actors for implementing and realizing of human rights (see Kirchschlaeger et al., 2005) or intergenerational justice. It becomes apparent that it is not appropriate from the perspective of a human rights holder, a victim of a human rights violation, or an object of intergenerational justice. For a human rights bearer, a victim of a human rights violation, or an object of intergenerational justice, the fulfillment of human rights, stopping a human rights violation or achieving intergenerational justice might also occur without the involvement or influence of an institution, an institutional system, or the global institutional system. Who the subject is does not change the importance and weight of the realization of human rights, intergenerational justice, or stopping a human rights violation because the essential elements and spheres of human existence protected by human rights are fundamental. From the perspective of a rights holder, a victim of a human rights violation, or an object of intergenerational justice, one understands the respective act as a realization of human rights or intergenerational justice or as a violation of human rights whether the particular act is official or not.

The practical potential of the institutional understanding of human rights and intergenerational justice makes a difference to theory and practice, but its exclusive priority is not demonstrable, as noted in the following: while Thomas Pogge emphasizes the individual responsibility of institutional decision makers, the same participation opportunity and sphere of influence can be claimed for individuals outside an institution – be it as political citizens, as political consumers (as "consumption-actors") (see Kirchschlaeger, 2016c), or others. The extension of a kind of "interactional understanding of human rights" that Thomas Pogge attributes to decision makers inside the inner workings of an institution and to individuals in the world outside an institution by virtue of their power and influence is possible and necessary so as not to underestimate the contribution of state and non-state actors. According to Thomas Pogge, the individual has an obligation in such a situation to either end his or her entanglement with the institution or to contribute to a corresponding reform of the institution (see Pogge, 2002, p. 48). There is an obligation to change the human rights situation if one has the power and influence to do so. It seems difficult to limit this assessment only to the inner workings of institutions, as individuals as political citizens as well as political consumers – as "consumption-actors" (see Kirchschlaeger, 2016c) – have power and influence on the realization of human rights or on intergenerational justice.

One might argue against this extension to state and non-state actors outside institutions that official actors must intervene in ways to avoid private human rights violations or make contributions to the realization of human rights and intergenerational justice. The assumption underlying this objection would presumably assume a rather broad understanding of the horizon of influence of institutions on an individual sphere of influence, which would go too far, as it would conflict with elements of the core of human rights itself, namely the autonomy of the individual.

Here, too, the institutional understanding of human rights or intergenerational justice highlights further central actors for the implementation and realization of human rights and intergenerational justice – institutions, institutional systems, and the global institutional system – that has not yet been the focus of discourse. Rather than ascribing primary or sole responsibility to those actors it seems more appropriate to assign primary responsibility for implementing and realizing human rights and intergenerational justice to states because of their enforceability, and to add to the actors who share the responsibility for the implementation and realization of human rights and intergenerational justice with states in particular non-state actors such as the private sector, civil society, individuals, institutions, institutional systems, and the global institutional system. The realization of intergenerational justice does not depend solely on adequate reforms of institutions, institutional systems, and the global institutional system, nor lies it solely in the hands of institutions, institutional systems, and the global institutional system; it depends on states (see Tremmel, 2006; Bourg, 2006; Shoham & Lamay, 2006; Jávor, 2006; van Opstal & Timmerhuis, 2006) and non-state actors such as the private sector, civil society, and individuals. A monitoring of the compliance with intergenerational justice by a global court of justice (see Brown, 1989, p. 121), or "a commission comparable to the UN Commission on Human Rights, without the power to impose sanctions, would also be helpful, able only to publicize and denounce violations of the interests of future generations, such as deforestation of rainforests, desertification, and greenhouse gas emissions" (Birnbacher, 2006, p. 37) is being contemplated.

Finally, intergenerational justice faces the following challenge: "One fact that complicates the practice of assuming responsibility for the future is the anonymity of future generations and the uncertainty of prognostic knowledge. Both facts make it easier for us to psychologically suppress recognized future dangers and to underestimate them in comparison to present dangers. The tendency to feel responsible for purely statistical casualties is much less pronounced than the tendency to feel responsible for known casualties. The tendency to avoid certain future harms or to reap certain future benefits is much more pronounced than the tendency to avoid risks or forego opportunities." (Birnbacher, 2006, p. 37) Also, this challenge is further supported by the objection that decisions and actions taken today do not affect future generations because only one's own actions determine who will live in the future, which we cannot know today (see Parfit, 1984, p. 367). The following rationale for human rights provides an ethical basis to which intergenerational justice can contribute for overcoming this challenge by providing “good reasons” (i.e., it must be conceivable that all people, in their effective freedom and autonomy, as well as their full equality would agree to these reasons – within a model of thought and not within a real worldwide referendum – on ethical grounds) for the ethical legitimacy of intergenerational justice and demonstrates the ethical necessity of respecting intergenerational justice and to decide and act for its realization. The latter also includes calling on all societal actors – state and non-state – to play their role according to their power and influence in achieving intergenerational justice.

Justice as a Principle for Ethical Decision-Making

Ethical decisions on the principle of intergenerational, omni-dynamic social justice open up the horizon for contributing to a world characterized by merit, fairness, reconciliation, need, equality, and sustainability, and particularly by an ethically based balance between merit, fairness, reconciliation, need, and equality.

Human Rights Principles

Human Rights – A Minimum Standard

Human rights (see Kirchschlaeger, 2018, 2019) make up a minimum standard that enables every human being to survive physically and to live with human dignity (see Kirchschlaeger, 2013e, p. 194f). It is surprising that this minimum standard is sometimes considered an ideal or even a utopia (see Moyn, 2010) because human rights are a rather minimalist approach. They protect only the physical survival and human dignity of all human beings. Human rights are neither maximal moral claims nor a higher ethos. This means that they do not overload ethical decisions with ethical claims. Rather, they prove to be realizable. Human rights have a precise focus that can promote clear prioritization based on minimum standards that must be met first. Therefore, they can help with agenda setting, establishing the right priorities, and appropriately defining spheres of influence and responsibility (see Kirchschlaeger, 2013e).

Characteristics of Human Rights

“All human beings are born free and equal in dignity and rights. They are endowed with reason and conscience and shall act towards one another in a spirit of brotherhood.” Article 1 of the Universal Declaration of Human Rights of 1948 (United Nations, 1948) expresses one of the eight essential characteristics of human rights : their *universality* (see Kirchschlaeger, 2011). Human rights are universal because all human beings are bearers of human rights – always, everywhere, and without exception. Without their universality, human rights would not provide all people with the necessary protection in all essential areas and elements protected by specific human rights.

Although there is a generally discernible positive trend in the acceptance of human rights by states and non-state actors, an increasing international institutionalization of human rights protection, progress in mechanisms for monitoring their observance by states, and some contributions by business in this area, it must be noted that their implementation is not yet where it should be. The vast majority of people still suffer from human rights violations. Human rights are still a minority phenomenon: only a minority of people enjoy human rights in full or in part. The difficulties in implementing them raise the question of whether human rights are achievable at all, whether they are not just abstract ideals, and whether some of them should be abandoned. As mentioned at the beginning of this chapter, some even refer to them as the "ultimate utopia" (Moyn, 2010). The *status quo* of the implementation of human rights does not do justice to the universality of them. This does not mean, of course, that human rights are not universal, because their universality is rooted in their moral dimension (see Kirchschlaeger, 2013a) and is therefore still valid. But it shows that there is an urgent need to implement human rights as rights that are not fully implemented and respected, as well as rights that in reality can lose their concrete meaning as well as ultimately their legal effect – both of which lead to their dissolution. This is difficult to imagine in the case of human rights, because they are a "monument" that cannot be overlooked and passed over without taking note of it (see Joas, 2011, p. 280).

In addition, there are critics in the human rights discourse who question the universality of human rights. They can be divided into three groups (see Lohmann, 2008a). The third challenge to the universality of human rights is a critical relativism based on skepticism about the low realization potential of human rights and the differences within that potential among the three categories of human rights. This critique cites the failure to realize certain human rights as a reason for removing them from the human rights catalog. Again, of course, a case can be made for why they cannot be deleted, but the very idea should be taken as a serious warning sign and an indication of problems. A positive change in favor of human rights lies primarily in the hands of those who – be they state or non-state actors – have more power and influence.

The concept of the universality of human rights is also influenced by their seven other essential characteristics: because of their *categorical nature*, they make all human beings unconditional bearers of human rights. In other words: no one has to fulfill any conditions or obligations to enjoy human rights (being human is enough).

But is it at all legitimate that human rights be associated with corresponding duties? Is it justified that all people are bearers of human rights that can, for example, restrict personal freedom because every bearer of rights must also respect the human rights of all other people? Do the specific human rights that restrict the actions of the individual have any legitimacy at all? Here, too, it becomes apparent that human rights need to be justified...

Human rights require a moral justification to prove their legitimacy and to remain coherent with their own core concept of autonomy of the individual because autonomy includes the claim to know the reason why one's own freedom should be restricted by human rights. These challenges lead to the question of how human rights can be justified. Every human being deserves to know the reason why he or she is the bearer of human rights and also the duty bearer of human rights, because the corresponding responsibility to respect the human rights of all other people restricts his or her freedom (see Kirchschlaeger, 2007a). Robert Alexy ties the existence of human rights exclusively to the possibility of their justification (see Alexy, 1998). The emphasis on the *status quo of human rights* as a historical, political, and legal consensus that enjoys global acceptance is not sufficient as a justification because of its descriptive and non-normative character and because of the particular origin of historical, political, and legal consensus in general.

The *equality of human rights* states that all people are equal bearers of these rights.

Moreover, they are constituted as *individual rights* and serve to protect the human being as an individual. This means that human beings as individuals are protected by human rights without having to be part of a particular collective.

However, seeing human beings as bearers of human rights does not mean that they are individualistic. Human rights are granted to all human beings on the basis of their human dignity, i.e., their status as human beings. That is, they are, *first,* not exclusive rights, but rights that every human being shares with all other human beings. In other words, human rights are not "Peter Kirchschlaeger rights", but human rights.

This leads us, *second,* to the duties that correspond to the human rights of every human being. The individual has to contribute to the realization of the human rights of all other human beings. This also means that the duties corresponding to one's own human rights or to the human rights of all other human beings limit the individual. The duties associated with human rights are to be understood as dynamic because depending on the context different behaviors are required of duty bearers so that the human rights of all other human beings are respected, protected, implemented, and realized (see Raz, 1986, pp. 170-171).

It should be mentioned here, however, that this is an "asymmetrical relationship" (Wolbert, 2003, p. 176) between rights and obligations. The human being is and always remains the bearer of human rights, regardless of whether he or she fulfills the duties corresponding to the human rights. "These rights are not forfeited by wrongdoing. A person does not need to prove him- or herself worthy of the granting of human rights." (Wolbert, 2003, p. 176)

In this context, James W. Nickel formulates the restriction that it is only fair if one has to choose between two bearers of human rights. to give preference to the one who is morally superior (see Nickel, 2015). The above-mentioned categorical character of human rights speaks against such a restriction: All people have an unconditional right to human rights.

A *third* argument against the suspicion that human rights are individualistic, is that rights always have a social character, since they regulate relations between at least two parties. This is shown, for example, by the fact that "rights establish duties towards others" (Raz, 1986, p. 167).

Fourth, Article 29 of the Universal Declaration of Human Rights of 1948 states: "Everyone has duties to the community in which alone the free and full development of his personality is possible." (United Nations, 1948, Art. 29) (see Kirchschlaeger, 2014b) Article 29 states that the individual can only develop in a collective and that he/she has duties towards this collective.

Fifth, individual rights and freedoms require a certain form of relationships and a certain social context for such universal cooperation between individual bearers of human rights who respect their rights to be conceivable at all (see also Gould, 2015).

Sixth, rights always have a social and not an "individualistic" component, since they must be part of a social system, because without at least a second person there would be no need for laws.

Furthermore, the *fundamental nature* as a characteristic of human rights indicates that human rights protect minimum standards – the essential elements and spheres of human existence necessary for survival and for a life as a human being, a life in human dignity – and do not represent a luxury.

Justiciability as a characteristic of human rights means that human rights are enforceable in a legal system.

And human rights are *inalienable rights*, that is, they can neither be acquired nor lost, and every human being is entitled to them (see Willoweit, 1992).

Finally, human rights must be thought of in their *multidimensionality* (see Kirchschlaeger, 2013d), as explained above: human rights contain a legal, a political, a moral, and a historical dimension. The universality of human rights can, however, be demonstrated in particular in their moral dimension.

In view of the current discourse on the universality of human rights one might get the impression that the term "universality" is the opposite of "relativism". In reality, however, the direct opposite of the first term would be "particularism,“ and "absolutism" would be the opposite of the second term (see Lohmann, 2008a). "The common view concludes that universalism can *only be* justified in absolute terms, and, if this is not possible, a merely relative justification leads to the abandonment of universalism and thus to a merely *particular* validity." (Lohmann, 2008a, p. 219, emphasis in original) This observation has bearing on the justification of human rights, which could well be relative according to this observation (see Lohmann, 2008a), but it can also show how to deal with the criticism of the universality of human rights which in most cases is based on individual positions and special interests.

The Need for an Ethical Justification of the Universality of Human Rights

The universality of human rights thus means that all people are bearers of human rights, regardless of what they do or not do, where they come from, where they live, what nationality they have, and what society and community they belong to.

The universality of human rights underscores the need for an ethical justification of human rights and their universality (see also Perry, 2005; Tasioulas, 2015) because people, societies, and communities demand reasons why human rights also apply to their societies, communities, institutions, and members. "Reasons are therefore between rights holders and the addressees of the obligations that stem from rights. Both sides will only be able to accept a justification if this relationality is also respected, and a justification seems to be an adequate one only if it applies to all concerned and generally to that extent." (Lohmann, 2000, p. 10)

If human rights are generally defensible rights, then any violation of human rights is no longer a generally defensible restriction on the self-determination of the individual or individuals (see Lohmann, 2000, p. 11).

Moreover, human rights indirectly protect diversity. However, they can protect it only if they themselves and their universal validity are also ethically justified. In respect to diversity the need for an ethical justification of human rights and their universality becomes obvious.

It can be argued against needing a justification of human rights in general that the phenomenon of human rights has already ensured that human rights are "un hecho-del-mundo" (Rabossi, 1990, p. 161) – a fact of the world. Therefore, the idea of an ethical basis or a moral justification of human rights is nowadays obsolete and no longer relevant (see Rabossi, 1990).

A counterargument to this position consists in the above-mentioned multidimensionality and the relationship between the human rights dimensions that require a justification of human rights because a purely legal understanding of human rights would be reductionist. A legal, political or historical justification of human rights alone would also miss its character, contradicting the argument described above. None of these justifications would in itself satisfy the claim to universality of human rights.

In addition, two further arguments could be made for the necessity of justifying human rights, both of which are rather weak in themselves: first, cultural, religious, and worldview-based diversity as a challenge to the universality of human rights shows the necessity of their ethical justification. Without an ethical justification, they would be void in cultural, religious, and worldview-based communities and would not be able to protect cultural, religious, and worldview-based difference, nor could they protect cultural, religious, and worldview-based communities in the service of respecting human rights – because without an ethical justification the boundaries of cultural, religious, and worldview-based communities would also be the boundaries of the validity of human rights (see Kirchschlaeger, 2013a, pp. 213-222).

On the other hand, practice shows that human rights can by no means be taken for granted. They still face major challenges and are in urgent need of justification, because in practice they are in danger when

- people do not know their rights, and human rights therefore remain an empty shell. "What is the use of having human rights when you don't know them, and what use is it to know them but not understand them? And finally: what good would it do if people only understood human rights, but were not prepared to respect them and stand up for them?" (Fritzsche, 2016, p. 181)
- human rights violations do not entail sanctions and thus diminish the weight, significance, and credibility of human rights, leading to their degeneration from rights to mere ideas in the sense of a reciprocal "customary law". The realization of the idea of human rights through international treaties (see Klein, 1997), which has been called the "silent revolution" of international law, threatens to stagnate. "If we put a high priority on the protection of rights, we should ensure that the institutions that are responsible for this protection are effective; otherwise, we are left with an element of prudential irrationality because we would have a clear goal with means that are incapable of achieving that goal." (Jones, 1999, p. 228)
- a no convincing justification can be given to sceptics: "The central idea of human rights as something that people have, even without specific legislation, is seen by many as fundamentally questionable and unconvincing. A recurring question is: where do these rights come from? [...] Concerns relate to the perceived 'softness' [...] of the conceptual basis of human rights." (Sen, 2004, p. 315)

Another argument against the need for a rationale for human rights consists of the position that the attempt to find a rationale for them is outdated. In a metaethical reflection it is argued that philosophy has the task of strengthening a culture of human rights rather than showing its superiority and universality to other cultures. Rationality is the act of striving for a coherent and intelligible structure of our beliefs. Philosophy can only hope to bundle culture-dependent intuitions by generalizing them to derive unassailable intuitions. These generalizations do not justify these intuitions, but summarise them, thereby increasing their predictability, power, and efficiency, as well as the sense of a shared moral identity of a moral society. Moving away from justifiability would be more efficient "because it would allow us to focus our energy on cultivating or educating feelings." (Rorty, 1996, p. 155)

This emphasis on intuition proposed by Richard Rorty raises the question whether this does not open the door to arbitrariness and irrationality. For both the affirmation and the denial of human rights could theoretically be attributed to intuitions, even if one must admit that the latter is difficult to imagine. Nevertheless, even in the first case, one would have to acknowledge the risks involved, which have serious implications for the understanding of human rights and human rights themselves. If they are simply taken as a given, they become absolute and forever immutable rights that require no justification. As a result, they would have an absolute and alternativeless validity, which would make them immune to religious and worldview-based differences and could lead to indoctrination. One could object that human rights understood in their multidimensionality as described above do not represent an absolute truth. Nor are they natural properties of human beings. They are a human construct. Human rights have developed historically. They are the result of a process of consensus among human beings. This consensus is based on reasons that together provide a rationale. If the human rights tradition does not discuss this rationale, it runs the risk of losing sight of the autonomous human being who has a right to address the question of justification because the need for justification is also based on the close connection between the idea of human rights and the idea of justification. "We would have no human rights at all if we did not understand human beings as bearers of rights in such a way that they would have to give reasons for everything that legitimately restricts them." (Lohmann, 2000, pp. 9-10) Every person as a bearer of human rights has a right to know why his autonomy is restricted through human rights and their corresponding duties. Because one has claims or rights that correspond to the duties of others. One not only has duties or obligations to others, and in this sense, one has a claim on them, but one also has the normative capacity to make claims on them. One can tell the oppressor that he/she has violated one's rights. If one is not a competent actor, others can make claims on his/her behalf (see Reeder, 2015, p. 100) This point can be summarized as "Justify what you are doing to me!" (Lohmann, 2000, p. 10) Human rights need a moral justification to prove their legitimacy and to be consistent with their own core concept of the autonomy of the individual because autonomy includes the claim to know the reason why one's own freedom is restricted by human rights.

Moreover, it is reductionist to try to reduce human beings to their intuition. The strong focus Richard Rorty places on intuition proves to be very relevant in the field of human rights education or advocacy for the promotion of human rights. At this point, however, Rorty confuses or reverses two levels. The assessment that intuition and feelings are very relevant in human rights education and in the engagement for the promotion of human rights should not be linked to a fundamental critique of the effort to justify human rights because this takes place at a different level than the level of human rights education or advocacy.

Finally, the question of the justification of human rights becomes even more relevant when, for example, it is tried to exclude a certain group of people from human rights in general or from some rights, when human rights in general are neglected or some rights are denied, or when state interventions violate certain human rights or may disregard them in general. In the face of these realities, reasons to justify human rights are necessary. An ethical model of their justification based on the principle of vulnerability helps to meet this challenge and shows that human rights can be ethically justified (see Kirchschlaeger, 2013a; Kirchschlaeger, 2016e; Kirchschlaeger, 2015a).

Ethical Justification of Human Rights on the Basis of the Principle of Vulnerability

Human rights can serve as an ethical principle that provides orientation for ethical decision-making because they can be justified ethically – e.g. through the principle of vulnerability (see Kirchschlaeger, 2013e, 2015b, 2016b). As an entry point into the ethical justification of human rights it is useful to examine the meta-question of what requirements an ethical justification of human rights must fulfill. An attempt to justify human rights must *first* answer the following two questions: why are all human beings bearers of human rights? Why are all human beings bearers of these specific human rights? (e.g., why can human rights not be claimed for other elements and areas of human existence?)

Second, the answers to these two questions must form a hermeneutic circle in which the answer to the question of how specific human rights are to be justified builds on the question of how human rights are to be justified in general.

Third, the attempt to justify human rights by these two complementary steps of justification must be suitable for a critical-rational ethics as defined in the introduction above. While justifying human rights and their universality it is also necessary "to free the understanding of human rights from the metaphysical ballast of the assumption of an individual given before all socialization who comes into the world with innate rights, as it were" (Habermas, 1999b, p. 399).

Fourth, an attempt at a justification must not only justify "human rights" in a first step, but must actually substantiate the following statements:

> "All people have the same human rights."
>
> "If someone is a human being, we grant him or her human rights."
>
> "All human beings are bearers of human rights."
>
> "All human beings are bearers of these specific human rights."

Fifth, an attempt at a justification must be designed in such a way that it can ethically justify in a second justification step that all human beings are bearers of specific human rights. The justification must therefore work for each individual human right.

The question of how the four statements above can be justified can be answered with the justification approach based on the principle of vulnerability. First of all, a distinction must be made between the terms "vulnerability" and the "principle of vulnerability". When a person becomes aware of his or her vulnerability he or she can become aware of the "first person perspective" and "self-relation". The principle of vulnerability encompasses the moral endeavor to protect the "first-person perspective" and the "self-relation" of all human beings in order to preserve the possibility of living as human beings.

The various reflections on this approach to the justification of human rights which are based on the principle of vulnerability include a first, second and third filtering step, which leads to an ethical justification of human rights in general and for specific human rights.

First Filtering Step

The justification on the basis of the principle of vulnerability is based on the observation that humans recognize their own vulnerability, a *first* element of this principle (see Kirchschlaeger, 2013a, pp. 231-267). For example, a person who is healthy today knows that he or she could become ill tomorrow. Or – while living happily in the present – that tomorrow he or she could be killed by others. In this thought process, the person goes through a process of uncertainty. For he or she becomes aware of his or her own vulnerability and, in the last consequence, of his or her transitoriness (see Hoffmaster, 2006, p. 42). This possibility of self-awareness applies to all people.

Second, an essential component of the principle of vulnerability is the "first-person perspective" (see Runggaldier, 2003). Becoming aware of one's own vulnerability is a self-awareness process of the person, the empirical accuracy of which is not relevant. What is decisive is that the person is willing to do something out of this awareness of his or her vulnerability, namely to protect him- or herself from it or to find a reasonable way of dealing with it. This also concerns all people.

During this process of becoming conscious, a person recognizes ex negativo the "first-person perspective" and the "self-relation". The "first-person perspective" includes a person's awareness that he or she is the subject of his or her own life experience, through which he or she has access to his or her own vulnerability (i.e., first person singular). The actions, decisions, sufferings, and the life of a person emanate from him or her as a subject. Furthermore, humans interpret this basic anthropological situation of vulnerability as a subject: "Because when acting and suffering he or she experiences him- or herself as the living being who does not simply live like all other living beings, but who lives only by leading *his or her life.* To relate to him- or herself, to act neither naturally nor arbitrarily, but to orientate him- or herself to reasons and to pursue freely chosen purposes, constitutes the form of life that connects him or her with all human beings as *his or her equals.* At the same time, it makes him or her vulnerable, since the self-relation belonging to his or her form of life is dependent on fundamental conditions of realization." (Honnefelder, 2012, pp. 171-172, emphasis in original) (The latter (see Hoeffe, 1991; Nussbaum, 1993) belongs to the two types of vulnerability presented above – the basic vulnerability and the selective and variable vulnerability – as well as to the inner and outer spheres and aspects of vulnerability and can occur in an inner and an outer form). In this process, the human being perceives "self-relation"; he or she relates to him- or herself.

Third, vulnerability is perceived by people from their "first-person perspective" as well as for the "first-person perspective" itself and "self-relation".

This process of becoming aware of one's own vulnerability and the "first-person perspective" leads *fourth* to the fact that the human being relates to all other human beings. In this process he or she recognizes that he or she is not different from other people because of his or her vulnerability, but that he or she shares this vulnerability with all people.

Fifth, the process of becoming aware of one's own vulnerability and the vulnerability of all other people enables people to perceive that they not only share the vulnerability with all other people, but also the individual "first-person perspective" on individual vulnerability and the vulnerability of all other people, as well as the individual "self-relation": each person is the subject of his or her own life. Humans therefore recognize that the "first-person perspective" and the "self-relation" are a condition for the possibility of a life as a human being.

Starting from the perception of vulnerability of their own "first-person perspective" and their own "self-relation", people become aware of the same vulnerability of all other human beings. People who first and foremost want to survive and live as human beings – with human dignity – become aware of the fact that the vulnerability affects both their own survival and the survival of all other people and also their own lives as human beings and the lives of all others as human beings, because vulnerability also affects the "first-person perspective" and the "self-relation" as conditions of the possibility of living as a human being. In the face of his or her own vulnerability the human being wants first and foremost to survive physically and to live a life worthy of a human being. Physical survival and a life worthy of a human being must not be taken away from the human being. They must be legally enforceable in order to offer real protection and they must be applicable to the various dimensions because vulnerability can include legal, political, historical, and moral dimensions. Physical survival and a life with human dignity should not be conditional because they are of utmost importance, as mentioned above, and because vulnerability is unpredictable. The desire to physically survive and live a life of human dignity is shared with all other human beings. This desire is not individualistic, even though it is a concern of each person as an individual, which each individual discovers through his/her "first-person perspective" and his/her "self-relation".

Sixth, because people are aware of their vulnerability but at the same time do not know if and when this vulnerability manifests itself and turns into a concrete violation or transgression, they are willing to grant all people the "first-person perspective" and "self-relation" based on the equality of all people, because this is the most rational, prudent, and advantageous solution for them. That means granting rights – human rights – to all people in order to protect themselves and all others, because the vulnerability also includes the "first-person perspective" and "self-relation". This protection through human rights aims, on the one hand, at avoiding the transformation of the vulnerability into a concrete violation and on the other hand - in case of such a transformation - to receive active compensation. In this context, people are aware that the protection through human rights also includes the duties corresponding to human rights, because they are not exclusive rights, but rights to which all people are entitled.

With regard to this sixth point, the question arises whether it is really rational, prudent, and advantegous to agree on human rights. For it is conceivable that a person because of his or her religious or worldview-based background may not shun vulnerability or injury, but may rather seek it, or that vulnerability is irrelevant for him or her (in their search for redemption). An argument against this objection would be that freedom of thought, conscience, and religion would also be vulnerable to violations. This means that even in this case it would be rational, prudent, and advantegous to plead for the protection through human rights.

One objection that would lead to further questions, however, would be that it is precisely this freedom of thought, conscience, and religion that could be a thorn in the side of a person who sees him- or herself as religious. In their eyes, this freedom would be superfluous, because it would not be a matter of seeking and finding the right religion, but the right religion would already be defined. Again, it could be argued that even if the right religion is already defined, freedom of thought, conscience, and religion will serve and be necessary for the life, cultivation, and practice of that religion.

Another argument against the sixth point of the first filtering step would be that, if one looks at the current implementation of human rights, one could conclude that it is disadvantageous for the individual to unilaterally agree on and comply with human rights. However, it could be argued that without human rights, the current situation would be even worse. Moreover, they are already a global consensus to which no similarly globally accepted alternatives are known and which already exists as an institution. Therefore, there seems to be no better alternative than human rights. Moreover, the unpredictability of the vulnerability or a possible transformation into a violation makes it seem irrational and disadvantageous to disregard human rights unilaterally.

It can also be objected that it is no longer reasonable to grant human rights to oneself and to everyone else and to comply with the agreed obligations if human rights are not enforced or do not entail sanctions when violated. Here, the unpredictability of vulnerability or a possible transformation of the same into a violation would serve as a counterargument. Because of the uncertain individual situation and perspective human rights, with their inherent justice, prove to be the best solution.

Furthermore, concerning the process of raising awareness of human rights described above, the question arises why humans should not choose another form of self-restraint or another way of dealing with this situation (e.g. violence, subordination, etc.). As explained above, human's primary concern is to survive and to live a life with human dignity. An argument in favor of human rights would be that they can best support this desire. Moreover, violence or subordination i.e. alternative forms of protection from vulnerability and violations that are based on inequality and injustice among people (e.g., the powerful and the powerless, the tyrant and the subordinate, the oppressor and the oppressed) and given the unpredictability of a possible transformation of vulnerability into injury are ruled out as rational, prudent, and advantageous alternatives because, due to this unpredictability, one does not know which side one stands or will stand on.

Finally, it should be explained at this point why it is conceivable or imaginable that e.g. also leaders or decision-makers are prepared to grant themselves and, on the basis of the equality of all people, all people the “first-person perspective” and “self-relation” as well as to protect themselves and all others through human rights. In the case of both, it can be assumed that they are also confronted with the vulnerability described above, that they are aware of it on the level of the individual, and that they are ready to address it on the basis of the principle of vulnerability. There are no "good reasons" why a leader or a decision-maker should be different from other people in this respect.

Of course, it is reasonable to assume that in the case of leaders or decision-makers their power and influence might mitigate their concern about vulnerability, but they would still experience vulnerability in certain elements and areas of human existence – even if it is only the fear of losing power that should remind them of their own vulnerability. Thus, in both cases, there are enough situations in which they might experience their own vulnerability which would influence their consent to create human rights based on the perception and awareness of the principle of vulnerability as well as the unpredictability of vulnerability introduced above or a possible transformation of vulnerability into a violation.

These six points on the principle of vulnerability explain that, *seventh,* vulnerability in itself has no moral quality, but the principle of vulnerability, the "first-person perspective", and "self-relation" as a moral claim is normatively charged. The principle of vulnerability concerns all human beings and distinguishes them from all other living beings, which is why human beings grant human rights to each other. Because they agree that they can prevent for themselves and all other human beings a transformation of vulnerability into a concrete violation or, in the case of a possible transformation of vulnerability into a concrete violation, an active compensation would be provided for all people. It would be a decision of the moral society that humans grant each other human rights according to the principle of vulnerability and make all people bearers of human rights.

People are not human rights bearers because of their vulnerability but because they deal with their own vulnerability and its relevance. They become aware of their own "first-person perspective" and "self-relation" and of all human beings and understand them as a condition of living as a human being. They even take on the vulnerability of the "first-person-perspective" and "self-relation" of all human beings because of the principle of vulnerability. People differentiate vulnerability based on experiences of injustice and injury and justify a protection of elements and areas of human existence based on the principle of vulnerability with specific human rights. The principle of vulnerability is therefore a starting point for the justification of human rights in general and of specific human rights.

Eighth: it is altogether possible that the principle of vulnerability can be the basis for recognizing new sufferings and experiences of injustice that, because of their threatening nature, require the protection through human rights. This need leads to formulating rights that go beyond the existing human rights. In this way, human rights remain open to new challenges that may arise. The principle of vulnerability contains a "discovery function" (Habermas, 2011a, p. 18) and leads to having to update and differentiate the human rights protection system.

These eight points form the first filtering step of the justification model based on the principle of vulnerability. Not all elements and spheres of human existence are eligible for protection by human rights only those which are based on the principle of vulnerability and which people want to use to protect themselves and others.

Second Filtering Step

The second filtering step builds on the above considerations and substantiates the areas of protection to which all human beings are entitled as bearers of human rights, because the consensus on the protection against vulnerability does not encompass all elements and spheres of human existence. But which elements and spheres of human existence should be protected by human rights? What criteria should be used to select these elements and areas of human existence?

The starting point are historical experiences of suffering and injustice to which people were subjected due to the principle of vulnerability or could be exposed to due to the principle of vulnerability. In view of these historically grave experiences of injustice and violence, and based on the principle of vulnerability people agree to prevent the transformation of vulnerability into concrete injury for themselves and all other and to provide for active compensation in the event of such a transformation.

Human rights protection does not apply to all historical experiences of injustice. It is necessary to select those that require human rights protection, which in turn requires criteria for this selection process. These can be derived from the above descriptions of people and the weighting because it shows what people want to protect themselves from. It sheds light on what criteria are needed for a historical experience of injustice to warrant a protection through human rights. First of all, people want to survive and live as human beings with human dignity (fundamentality). People become aware that their vulnerability threatens their own survival and the survival of all human beings as well as their own life as human beings living with human dignity and the lives of all others as human beings living with human dignity (universality), because vulnerability does not stop at the "first-person perspective" and "self-relation" as a condition of living as a human being. Survival and a dignified life must not be taken away from people (inalienability). They must be legally enforceable (justiciability) and applicable to the different dimensions (multidimensionality) because vulnerability can include legal, political, historical, and moral dimensions. Because they possess such a high priority, as mentioned above, and because vulnerability is unpredictable and can be transformed into injury, survival and a dignified life should not be conditional (categorical character). People share this desire to survive and live a decent life with all other people (equality) to the same extent. It is not individualistic, even though each individual discovers it through his or her own "first-person perspective" and "self-relation" (individual validity). Therefore, the following eight criteria determine the selection of those historical injustices and vulnerabilities from which all human beings should be protected by specific human rights: fundamentality, universality, inalienability, justiciability, multidimensionality, categorical character, equality, and individual validity.

The second filtering step filtering the justification model based on the principle of vulnerability characterizes an inherent openness to new threats, risks, and experiences of injustice that are currently non-existent or cannot be imagined, as well as an openness to experiences of injustice that occur in different religions, cultures, traditions, civilizations, and worldviews.

At the same time, the second filtering step addresses the challenges of applying these eight criteria to historical experiences of injustice, such as the challenges of historical contingency and the universalization of certain experiences of injustice.

Third Filtering Step

This step involves applying the above-mentioned eight criteria to identify the elements and spheres of human existence that must be protected by human rights.

The criterion of "fundamentality" is met when a historical experience of injustice touches an element or area of human existence necessary for physical survival or life as a human being.

In order for the criterion of "universality" and the above-mentioned challenge of historical contingency and universalization of particular experiences of injustice to be met, rational reasons are needed as to why an experience of injustice is relevant to human rights and touches on an element or area of human existence that must be protected for everyone, everywhere, and always. Rational reasons are necessary to enable the transition from a subjective experience of injustice or violation to a universal experience of injustice or violation (see Hoernle, 2011, p. 67).

The criterion of "inalienability" presupposes that the right corresponding to a particular element or sphere of human existence can neither be acquired nor lost, and that every human being is entitled to this right.

The criterion of "justiciability" is met if the relevant right can be enforced in a legal system.

The criterion of "multidimensionality" is met if it can be thought of in terms of legal, political, moral, and historical dimensions.

As for the criterion of "categorical character", it must be shown that humans do not have to do anything in order to have this vulnerability or injury or the corresponding right which protects against this vulnerability or injury.

In order for the criterion of "equality" to be met, everyone must be able to enjoy the corresponding right without distinction.

The criterion of "individual validity" is fulfilled if an individual can have the corresponding right independently of a collective.

A rationale for human rights and its universal validity must be formulated in such a way that it not only substantiates human rights in itself, but can also be checked against each individual human right. The justification of human rights on the basis of the principle of vulnerability can be applied to each individual human right, as has already been shown with some examples (see Kirchschlaeger, 2013e, pp. 290-335, 2015b).

Universal Human Rights Protect Against Exclusion

On this ethical basis, human rights represent a universal consensus. The latter means that no other set of norms is globally accepted to the same extent. They have credibility and represent a globally respected ethical standard.

Also, human rights are not based on a particular tradition, culture, religion, worldview, or value system. (see Gut, 2008; Joas, 2015; Kirchschlaeger, 2016d). Human rights offer "a common basis for a humane existence beyond ideological differences" (see Habermas, 1999a, 2001, p. 125).

From particular perspectives attempts are made to violate human rights in general, some human rights, human rights of some people in general, or some human rights of some people out of self-interest. Human rights in their universality protect against this exclusion.

Universal Human Rights Promote Plurality

Human rights have not simply "fallen from the sky", but have grown historically – out of specific contexts and mostly as a reaction to injustice with universal validity. A selective view of their historical development taking into account only "western" sources, has been broken down and transformed into recognizing the contributions to human history from different traditions, cultures, religions, worldviews, philosophies, civilizations, and value systems, from different states as well as from the international community at large (see Kirchschlaeger, 2016d). Human rights are on the rise and are a consensus that has emerged through history and is open to further development depending on history. The human rights tradition and its continuation make history. Humanity faces new challenges. Hitherto unknown dangers threaten basic elements of human existence (see Kirchschlaeger, 2016e). It is inevitable that we react to it to protect the human dignity of each and every individual.

A historical classification of human rights must be appropriately categorized in terms of its contribution to human rights. It focuses on the genesis of human rights, while the discourse of justification focuses on the validity of human rights. Based on these considerations, approaches that use specific historical events as connecting factors for justifying human rights reach their argumentative limits, because this argument runs counter to their universality. At the same time, the historical contingency of human rights contributes greatly to their understanding. Based on historical experiences of injustice, people have endowed each other with human rights. This continues to shape them to the present day in the sense that they aim to end injustice and that they must be fought for again and again. Neither the temporal nor the geographical setting of the emergence of human rights is decisive for their normative validity today. Rational reasons are decisive. Similar to other theories, what matters most is whether human rights are rationally convincing and plausible, i.e., whether "good reasons" speak for them. When considering Albert Einstein's theory of relativity, does it matter when and where it was developed? Probably not. What matters is whether or not the theory of relativity can be disproved. Does the fact that Immanuel Kant developed the categorical imperative in Koenigsberg more than 200 years ago make his theory more or less convincing?

Concerning the universality of human rights even their historically contingent origin is not an argument for or against them. Because also in this case the rational reasons for the human rights justification (e.g. on the basis of the principle of vulnerability) and the resulting ethical irrelevance of the historically contingent origin of human rights for their claim to universality needs to be pointed out. At the same time, the contingent temporal and geographical origins of human rights do not prevent their universality.

Finally, the universality of human rights ensures that every human being is free and autonomous. Thanks to the freedom and autonomy of each individual diversity can emerge because each person is free to understand him- or herself as he or she wishes and to shape his or her life according to his or her freedom and autonomy. In this way, universal human rights protect and promote plurality (see Kirchschlaeger, 2020a, 2020b).

Human Rights as Principles for Ethical Decision-Making

Human rights protect what is necessary for survival and for a dignified life – a life as a human being. They thus form a minimum ethical standard that does not overtax ethical decision-making, but rather provides a clear focus, prioritization and a fundamental orientation.

As an ethical reference point for ethical decision-making, they are therefore at the same time very realistic and have a practical orientation. They are highly applicable to the real world and provide concrete ethical guidelines for ethical decision-making. Compared to other ethical principles, human rights encompass not only the ethical but also the legal dimension: they are legally defined, have a legal framework and are enforceable. Institutions such as the UN Human Rights Council and the UN High Commissioner for Human Rights in Geneva and the regional mechanisms for the protection of human rights on the various continents are elements for realizing their idea and can promote their culture (see Kirchschlaeger, 2022). They show that they are *real* and not an illusion. Human rights are a legal reality in all parts of the world.

It is obvious that their enforcement is facing challenges everywhere. But the legal mechanisms, instruments, and human rights institutions give the idea of human rights as the epitome of the protection of human dignity a clear face. Approaching this legal dimension from the local level makes it possible to begin in the context of the addressees and to enable them to approach human rights from their real experience and from their understanding of justice, freedom, and equality – always taking into account the universal dimension of human rights.

In addition, human rights as a principle for ethical decision-making have the advantage that they are inherently linked to their legal dimension, which serves as the basis for complying with legal standards. This aspect should not be misunderstood as neglecting the difference between legal compliance and ethics.

Furthermore, a global society is composed of different traditions, cultures, religions, worldviews, and value systems. This heterogeneity is protected by human rights. At the same time, they give this heterogeneity clear boundaries that must be respected: even within traditions, cultures, religions, worldviews, and value systems, human rights protect the elements and spheres of human existence essential for physical survival, as well as human dignity. Therefore, as a principle, they can guide ethical decision-making when faced with the opportunities and challenges of tradition, culture, religion, worldview, and value systems. (see Kirchschlaeger, 2013c).

Human rights are a universal consensus, which gives greater weight to this ethical principle for ethical decision making, as it is not based on a particular tradition, culture, religion, worldview, or value system. This becomes clear when considering the discussion of, for example, the process of creating the Universal Declaration of Human Rights of 1948. Jacques Maritain reports that the drafters refused to base human rights on a single tradition, culture, religion, worldview, or value system – out of respect for the universality of human rights and for cultural, religious, and worldview-based diversity, and plurality: "Yes, we agree on rights, but only on the condition that no one asks us why" (Maritain, 1948; see Kirchschlaeger, 2015a, 2016d).

Human rights as an ethical instrument free the subject taking ethical decisions from the suspicion of arbitrariness in his or her ethical self-commitment, because they are a widely recognized ethical standard.

Another pragmatic reason for their validity stems from the process of drafting the legal human rights treaties based on the Universal Declaration of Human Rights of 1948. It consists of the following idea, which was already in people's minds at that time and which influenced the drafting of the human rights documents: "The members of the Commission must take into account the fact that their work concerns the future and not the past." (United Nations, 1950). Human rights prove to be future-oriented and future-proof.

In addition, the dynamic nature of human rights must be emphasized at this point. They have always been open to adaptation in order to stop and prevent new risks, dangers, and violations of human dignity. Therefore, they are also ready to adapt to future challenges (see Kirchschlaeger & Kirchschlaeger, 2010).

Furthermore, ethical decisions are protected by human rights in essential areas and elements of human existence that human beings need to survive and live as human beings. Some of them are of particular importance for ethical decision-making processes, e.g., the right to freedom (Art. 2); the right to freedom of thought, conscience, and religion (Art. 18); the right to freedom of opinion and the freedom of opinion and expression (Art. 19); the right to participate freely in the cultural life of the community, to enjoy the arts, and to share in scientific advancement and its benefits (Art. 27(1)), as set forth in the Universal Declaration of Human Rights of 1948 (United Nations, 1948).

Limits of one's own human rights are first of all – in the case of a specific human right – *the other specific human rights* according to the principle of indivisibility. This principle states that all human rights must go hand in hand. This means that the entire catalog of human rights must be respected. Therefore, each human right must be realized as well as possible and in accordance with all other human rights, which are also implemented as well as possible. Second, one's own human rights are limited by the *human rights* of *all other human beings*. For example, one's own right to freedom applies only so far as it is compatible with the right to freedom of all other people. Both limits also result in corresponding duties for a right bearer, which is why every right bearer is also a duty bearer (see Corillon, 1989; Kirchschlaeger, 2014a).

These duties can be negative (*not doing something* to contribute to the realization of human rights) or positive *(doing something* to contribute to the realization of human rights).

GUIDELINE

D. *How can you ethically justify the ethical points of reference you have chosen?*

TARGET

The goal is to rationally and ethically justify out of respect for the plurality of ethics why one has chosen this/these ethical reference point(s) and why other ethical principles/norms/standards/theory/approaches are not considered.

The selection of the ethical reference point(s) should be free from arbitrariness, sympathies, emotions, as well as gut feeling, but should be rationally justifiable and plausible. "Also, decisions between ethical theories and methods are reasonable to the extent that good reasons can be given for them – something that can be used to argue in favor of what is defended in each case. Insofar as certain reasons for their part can only be convincing within a certain framework (on the basis of certain premises, certain methods, or within certain theoretical presuppositions), reasons can be asked for again within that framework. With respect to ethical approaches, talking of the choice of theory and method does not have to be understood as a final decision that can no longer be reasonably made ('decisionistic'), as long as it has not already been shown that, on the one hand, no further reasons can be given (e.g., because we have arrived at final axioms) and that, on the other hand, meaningful, seriously defensible alternatives to the theory or method to be defended are at all available" (Werner, 2021, p. 239f). This rational justification with "good reasons" is all the more necessary as one strives for universal validity. "Moral standards should be universal and take precedence over other practical standards (mores, social conventions, cultural practices, and customs). Basic moral standards should also guide legal frameworks" (Pauder-Studer, 2020, p. 14).

When justifying the selection of the ethical reference point(s), the principle of generalizability must be fulfilled by presenting rational and plausible arguments – "good reasons" – for it. "Good reasons" means that it must be conceivable that all human beings in their effective freedom and autonomy as well as their full equality, would agree to these reasons – within a model of thought and not within a real worldwide referendum – on ethical grounds (see Kirchschlaeger, 2021a).

Moreover, ethical justifications are to be differentiated from moral justifications, which refer to a fact, to feelings, to possible consequences, to a moral code, to moral competence, or to the conscience. (see Pieper, 2017, pp. 149-171) Ethical justifications, on the other hand, include the "logical method. All methods of ethics, insofar as they are to lead to scientific results, must satisfy the criteria of formal logic, and in this broad sense, every ethical method is also a logical method. In a narrower sense, one can speak of a logical method of ethics where it develops a 'deontic logic' (from Greek *to deon* – the intended, the duty) in order to show consistent and non-contradictory relations between any normative propositions" (Pieper, 2017, p. 172).

Furthermore, it includes the "discursive method". "Such claims to validity, which are always made inexpressively in action-related judgments, are subjected to a critique in a practical discourse. Discursive means: unquestionably recognized norms and values with regard to their general bindingness. On the *first* level of argumentation of the practical discourse, the participants in the discourse question their claims to validity. The positions of the opponents are clarified in speech and counter-speech and the reasons for the respective assessment of the behavior in question are given. [...] On the *second* level of argumentation of the practical discourse the participants in the discourse reach a consensus that is not a mere coincidence and thus binding only on them, but to which every other person, provided he or she is reasonable and of good will, must also be able to agree" (Pieper, 2017, p. 179, emphasis in original).

In addition, there is the "dialectical method": "In the form of speech and counter-speech it is attempted to come to an understanding about what is to be done or which norms can rightfully lay claim to general validity. Dialogue thus has a mediating function, it mediates between normative and factual claims by constantly arguing back and forth between the two. In the process, the factual is to be changed in such a way that it satisfies the claim of the norm, and the norm is to be concretized in such a way that it becomes effective as a regulator of action in the factual" (Pieper, 2017, p. 182).

The "analogical method" can also help: "The analogical method developed by moral prudence (phronesis) to determine what is good in each case by determining what is wanted as the proper middle ground between two extremes, both of which miss the moral mark insofar as they either remain below the mark or overshoot it and insofar represent deformities of human behavior" (Pieper, 2017, p. 189).

The "transcendental method" is also a method among the ethical justifications: "The transcendental method (from Latin *transcendere* – to go over, to exceed) is a reductive procedure, i.e., it traces moral action back to the constitutive conditions of its possibility by reconstructing the genesis of the concept of morality to its unconditional origin. This reconstruction, which unfolds the implications of the concept of morality a priori in such a way that a logical series of concepts emerges, in which the conditional is regressively inferred from the conditional and leads to an unconditional beginning that is itself no longer conditional, no longer questionable, and that is at the same time the unsurpassable ultimate ground and the highest norm of all (morally justified) ought." (Pieper, 2017, p. 190f)

Furthermore, ethical justifications also include the "analytic method": "Just as every methodological procedure must formally satisfy the demands of logic, no ethical procedure can do without analysis, insofar as a complex object can only be represented by a conceptual dissection of the moments it contains. In this sense of a conceptually dissecting procedure, dissecting a complex phenomenon into its implicit partial moments, every ethical method is at the same time an analytical procedure" (Pieper, 2017, p. 193).

Finally, the "hermeneutic method" belongs to the ethical justifications. "The *hermeneutic* method (from the Greek *hermeneuein* – to interpret, to explain), as it has been developed mainly by Hans-Georg Gadamer in following Martin Heidegger, elevates the historicity of understanding to the principle of interpretation. It emphasizes the importance of tradition through which the interpreter's preconceptions are as much predetermined as the interpreter reinterprets them in the horizon of meaning of his expectations and integrates them into his self-understanding. The hermeneutic method, too, is a procedure that every ethics must use to a certain extent, namely wherever it has to deal with ethically relevant statements that have to be interpreted, be it that these statements are available in the form of texts of other moral philosophers, be it that they are part of the argument of the discussion partner in a conversation: Each time, foreign statements have to be appropriated in an understandable way, which is only possible within the horizon of an already existing pre-understanding of meaning. In order to be able to claim meaning, meaning must already be understood. In order to understand meaning, one must always have made claims to meaning. Hermeneutics is concerned with the elucidation of the historical mediatedness of moral self-understanding" (Pieper, 2017, p. 196f, emphasis in original).

GUIDING QUESTION:
E. *How would you define the ethical question/challenge/problem?*

GOAL:
The goal is to define the ethical question/challenge/problem with the help of ethically grounded ethical reference point(s).

Rationally and ethically grounded clarity regarding ethical reference point(s) now allows the ethical question/challenge/problem to be carefully, conscientiously, and precisely identified.

This process of defining the ethical question/challenge/problem is furthered by "*ethical situation hermeneutics*: the collaboration of individual disciplines cannot be exhausted in bringing together empirical and normative elements like building blocks that are subsequently assembled. This can be illustrated as follows: an essential element of ethical judgment about situations or types of situations lies in exploring a problem interpretively. It seems that the morally relevant aspects of the situation must first be perceived as such before situational ethical questions can be posed, broken down into empirical and normative aspects, and processed. In reality, however, the supposedly preparatory situational inference always implies a preliminary and maybe only implicit judgment process that relates normative and empirical assessments to one another. Only in the light of normative presuppositions do certain observations stand out from the irrelevant background and do certain empirical questions become significant; only certain observations and empirical presuppositions justify the assumption that a certain morally relevant case might exist. What is more, the hope of being able to work through normative and empirical questions separately after the situation has been interpreted is usually deceiving. Because, as a rule, new or more specific factual insights give rise to further normative questions and require new or more precise normative findings for further empirical clarification. The interdisciplinary cooperation that is characteristic of ethics discourses therefore usually takes place as an *iterative process in* which empirical and normative-ethical questions and insights must be repeatedly related to each other. This dialogue presupposes translation competencies on both sides" (Werner, 2021, p. 249, emphasis in original). The ethical question/challenge/problem that emerges in the process must be answered or mastered in the course of ethical decision-making.

6.3 Be the Ethical Judge!

GUIDING QUESTION:
A. *What is your ethical assessment?*

GOAL:
The goal is to take a position from an ethical standpoint and make an ethical evaluation. This ethical position and ethical evaluation can initially include both a response and a mastery of the challenge as well as the problem, and subsequently a concrete ethical proposal for a solution.

Making ethical judgments is a challenging task. "The detailed definition of the standards of right and good is controversial. Nevertheless, there is a consensus about the subject matter of morality. Moral questions arise in the context of vulnerability, pain, suffering, inequality, and oppression" (Pauder-Studer, 2020, p. 14). It is helpful if the person who has to make an ethical decision is aware of the following: "Our starting point, then, is the observation that each of us from time to time experiences a gap, a discrepancy between what is good and what only appears to be good. This own experience of discrepancy is from the outset something different than a *claim* brought in solely from the outside, from other people, that something that is demanded of them is good in contrast to what is immediately desired (the child should sleep, but it wants to play). It is about the own experience of a discrepancy (I wanted to play, but it is good to sleep). Such experiences cannot be provided to anyone by talking, the most one can do is remind them of it" (Hastedt, 1994, p. 17, emphasis in original).

Taking an ethical position in the sense of an ethical decision has to fulfill certain requirements. "Given the complexity of the current problem and the openness of the valid orientations, however, the unavoidable ethical discussions cannot be decided according to instinct or with the simple mind of a good person, but require some knowledge and skills" (Hastedt, 1994, p. 7). In the course of this, we should be aware of one characteristic of ethics. "Maybe ethics *is* often uncertain and untestable. But maybe that isn't such a bad thing. It does not follow, in any case, that we should strive to make decisions in 'value-free' ways instead, for example, by scientific or economic or other 'practical' standards. The reason is that we *can't*. There simply is no such thing as 'value-free' decision making. Instead, all decision making – indeed, one could argue, all action – is *value-laden* (as it's often put). Indeed, any time we choose to do one thing rather than another, or anything at all rather than nothing, we are acting on certain values and leaving others to the side. When the needs and legitimate expectations of others as well as ourselves are at stake, the values involved are ethical by definition. The only question is how explicit and deliberate we are going to be about them." (Weston, 2017, p. 488, emphasis in original)

Against this background, a differentiation between "is" and "ought" is possible. "The distinction between facts and values is a characteristic of the philosophy of modernity. Both Hume and Kant were pioneering for this distinction. But while Hume limited the possibility of rationality to theoretical rationality (correspondence of beliefs and facts), Kant distinguished between theoretical reason which allows for the knowledge of facts, and practical reason, which examines maxims of action for their universalizability" (Nida-Ruemelin, 2005a, p. 46f). This universalizability, which is demonstrated by fulfilling the principle of generalizability, has to be shown in the ethical evaluation. "In 'Morality as a System of Hypothetical Imperatives' [Foot, Philippa: Virtues and Vices. Berkeley 1978], Philippa Foot distinguishes between two different 'uses' of 'ought' in judgments about what others ought to do: the *hypothetical* use, which presupposes that the subject of the judgment has a desire or interest, broadly understood, that would be served by his doing as we judge he ought; and the *categorical* use, which makes no such presupposition. For example, when we say someone 'ought to leave now, to catch the 6 o'clock train,' we presume that she wants to be on that train. If we learn she is really headed somewhere else, we withdraw the judgment. But moral judgments aren't like that: we don't, for example, withdraw our judgment that Hitler ought not to have issued his terrible orders when we learn that they fit perfectly into his plans." (Markovits, 2014, p. 16, emphasis in original) Here, the focus of ethics and thus the focus of ethical decision-making becomes visible: "For the clarification of concrete ethical problems, there is often a multitude of empirical and prognostic questions to be answered. The focus of ethical reflection, however, is not the descriptive and explicative preoccupation with moral questions, but the generation, verification, and substantiation of *normative* statements. Ethics – understood as *normative* ethics – does not ask primarily about what is, but about what should be *done*. Such ought-statements, however, have a different status with regard to eudaimonistic questions than in the field of discussion of normative questions. Whereas *evaluative* statements, which are always dependent on certain conceptions of the good and successful life, have only the status of *advice* or *recommendations*, norms or principles of the morally right raise a universal and categorical claim to validity, which – as soon as it can be reasonably justified – gives them priority over all other practical considerations" (Duewell & Huebenthal, 2011, p. 2, emphasis in original).

Within the categorical use of the ought and thus of ethical evaluation, one can start from the following basic categories, which can be helpful in ethical decision-making: "Basic categories of the moral evaluation of actions are the categories of the morally forbidden, the morally permitted, and the morally demanded as well as the corresponding subcategories. These categories are basic because the moral evaluation of actions always presupposes that what is morally forbidden can be distinguished from what is morally permitted and morally demanded – irrespective of what substantive standard of moral rightness it applies, what reasons for moral ought it assumes, and what normative ethic it is based on" (Stoecker, 2011, p. 13f).

But this is not sufficient. "A simple trichotomous model, as suggested by deontic logic – the logic of the ought or of normative propositions – does not do justice to the differentiating power of our moral judgment. As moral judges, if the action to be judged seems neither morally reprehensible nor morally required, we are hardly ever satisfied with assigning it to the third basic category provided by deontic logic. For this category includes both actions that, although not morally required, are morally very desirable, and actions that, from a moral standpoint, are neither reprehensible nor desirable, and it is part of the practice of moral judgment to distinguish between these two kinds of actions. The category of the morally permissible therefore requires an internal differentiation between the morally desirable and the morally neutral [...]. A further internal differentiation is obvious for the subcategory of morally desirable acts. A morally desirable act can be morally inappropriate for different reasons: it can be an act that is morally desirable, but whose omission cannot be regarded as morally reprehensible even if performing the act seems reasonable to the actor. However, it may also be an act that is morally desirable but cannot be expected of the potential actor because it would demand more of him/her than morality may reasonably demand of him/her. If an actor performs such a supererogatory action that exceeds what is morally demanded, as is the case according to the conviction of some authors, with a living organ donation [...], he or she acts as a 'moral hero', i. e. in a way that demands special admiration or respect from us and that therefore cannot be assigned to the same basic category without a corresponding qualification as, for example, picking up a hitchhiker on a balmy summer night, which will generally be regarded as 'merely' a morally desirable act" (Stoecker, 2011, p. 15f).

Furthermore, there should be an additional differentiation on our radar, which opens up another field for ethical evaluation: "There are two conceptual registers in which we broach the issue of moral facts – the deontic (i.e., concepts of duty and ought) and the evaluative (i.e., notions of good and bad). It is obvious that these two domains or registers do not exist completely unrelated to each other. It has already become clear that the category of a normative reason maintains intensive relations to both" (Henning, 2019, p. 40). These also bring challenges for ethics, which ethical decision-making has to take into account in order to respect the plurality of ethics. "The increasing differentiation between *evaluative* questions of the good life and *normative* questions of what is morally right is closely interrelated with the pluralization of concepts of the good life and the secularization of state authority. If a uniform, widely shared concept of the good life is replaced by a *plurality of the different*, often contradictory concepts of the good, ethics must also address the question of how the resulting conflicts of values and interests can be peacefully and justly resolved. The question of the *just settlement of conflicts of values and interests* is the subject of a separate reflection on what is *morally right*. Since modern times, this question has increasingly come to the forefront of ethical reflection efforts and appears to dominate the current context of discussion as well" (Duewell & Huebenthal, 2011, p. 1f, emphasis in original).

In addition, ethical evaluation informs to keep in mind the following three possible moral orientations that can influence us when making ethical judgments:

- "*Legalism:* the legalist appeals first to laws and principles when required to make a moral decision" (Gillmore & Hunter, 1974, p. 3, emphasis in original).
- "*Antinomianism:* This is the approach with which one enters into the decision-making situation armed with no principles or maxims whatsoever, to say nothing of rules. In every 'existential' moment or 'unique' situation, it declares, one must rely upon the situation of itself, there and then, to provide its ethical solution." (Gillmore & Hunter, 1974, p. 3, emphasis in original).
- "*Situationism:* The Situationist is characterized by his emphasis on human welfare. The Situationist enters into every decision-making situation fully armed with the ethical maxims of his community and its heritage, and he treats them with respect as illuminators of his problems. Just the same he is prepared in any situation to compromise them or set them aside *in the situation* if love seems better served by doing so." (Gillmore & Hunter, 1974, p. 4, emphasis in original)

The "rule-transcending uniqueness of the concrete" introduced above in chapter 5 can help here with regard to the three possible moral orientations as a concept. The rule-transcending uniqueness of the concrete means that ethical principles, norms, and values can collide or diverge in a concrete encounter with concrete persons in a concrete situation, and that in a concrete encounter with concrete persons in a concrete situation rules can reach their limits because the concrete in its uniqueness can surpass the rule, and it can be the ethically right and ethically good in a concrete encounter with concrete persons in a concrete situation to disregard an ethical principle, an ethical norm, or an ethical value in the service of the ethically right and ethically good. Ethical principles, norms, and values do not thereby lose their validity, but are affirmed by this striving for the ethically right and ethically good in a concrete encounter with concrete persons in a concrete situation. This ensures that the ethical principles and norms serve people and not vice versa.

Finally, the formation of ethical judgment is characterized by the fact that it itself forms a process and moves itself towards an action that corresponds to it. "Ethics is not understood as a justification of what is, but of what will become. It emerges from a process of forming a judgment" (Kolster, 2006, p. 122).

GUIDING QUESTION:
B. *How can you justify your ethical assessment?*

GOAL:
The aim is to justify the ethical position and the ethical evaluation rationally and ethically. In this justification, the principle of generalizability must be satisfied by listing "good reasons" for doing so. "Good reasons" means that it must be conceivable that all human beings in their effective freedom and autonomy as well as their full equality would agree to these reasons – within a model of thought and not within a real global referendum – on ethical grounds (see Kirchschlaeger, 2021a).

In order to rationally justify and make the universality of the ethical evaluation plausible, reasons and arguments need to be listed to support the ethical judgment, which fulfill the principle of generalizability. The latter can also be captured as follows: "If a moral judgment is true in a particular situation, then the judgment is also true in every situation that is the same in morally relevant respects" (Pfister, 2013, p. 134).

Such reasons and arguments can be characterized as follows: "An *argument* is a statement or a group of statements with which the *claim to validity* of an assertion is substantiated. Contrary to 'asking' or 'commanding', 'asserting' always involves the claim that what is said applies and is true or correct. Descriptive statements of fact such as 'At the moment the sun is shining' are associated with the claim to *truth*, i.e. that this statement corresponds to the objective fact that the sun appeared. In the field of ethics however, assertions in the form of normative statements such as 'You should help this old lady' do not, strictly speaking, make a claim to truth, but to *normative correctness:* it is asserted that it is morally correct or demanded in the given situation to help the old lady. By making an assertion one assumes at the same time the duty to defend it argumentatively when asked. The argument is thus something that is put forward as justification or proof for an opinion or a point of view. In short, it is a justifying statement or a reason for proof. As a consequence, to argue is to give reasons for or against a particular position [...]. Formally, every argument consists of two elementary building blocks: 1. *conclusion,* i.e., the claim or position to be justified, and 2. *premises, i.e.,* the statements that support or justify this conclusion" (Fenner, 2020, p. 63f, emphasis in original).

This listing of reasons and arguments – the arguing – can also be subjected to a differentiation, which proves to be reaching further: "1. According to the *rhetorical* approach, the function of arguing is to make an addressee believe something. It does not matter whether what is believed is true, but only that the addressee afterwards believes the thesis of the person arguing. (Rhetoricians often even doubt that there is such a thing as truth at all). 2. *The consensus theory* approach sees the function of arguing to bring about consensus. Again, what matters is not truth, but that there is agreement. 3. According to the *epistemological* approach, the function of arguing is to produce knowledge in the strict sense; this is a belief that is so well founded as to be *rationally acceptable,* i.e.: true, probably true, or truth-like. Knowledge is a compellingly grounded true belief. *Cognitions* include knowledge, but also rationally acceptable beliefs with flimsier reasons that are substitutes for knowledge sought when, given the current state of information, knowledge cannot be obtained or can be obtained only at too great a cost. Reasoning that leads to knowledge is said to be rationally *persuasive*" (Ach et al., 2011, p. 123, emphasis in original).

If, in the course of arguing for an ethical evaluation, attention is now given to the construction and unfolding of a rationale or line of argument, one has numerous argumentative options at the disposal:

"*Subordination to a standard*

If one wants to argue for the fact that in a certain situation a certain behavior is demanded, forbidden or permitted, it is obvious that one would resort to a norm which can be applied to a particular behavior that falls in that particular situation. One could argue as follows:

1. It is morally forbidden to kill an innocent human being.
2. *The human fetus is an innocent human being.*
3. It is morally forbidden to kill a human fetus.

In this way, one does not commit a being-ought fallacy, since one relies on a proposition (the first premise) that is already normative. However, it is possible that in a discussion one commits the fallacy of a *petitio* with such an argument [...], because in the first premise one already presupposes something that the discussion partner is putting into question.

Analogy

An important form of argument in ethics is the argument by analogy [...]. Let us consider the following argument:

1. We are to help a drowning child.
2. With regard to the drowning child, we are in a similar *situation as with regard to this beggar here.*
3. We are to help this beggar.

The first sentence is a normative statement. The second establishes an analogy between the first situation and a second situation. It is concluded that a corresponding normative statement also holds in this other situation." (Pfister, 2013, p. 129ff, emphasis in original; see also Fenner, 2020, p. 75f)

"*Demand of good consequences*

One should do what has morally good consequences as long as one does not have to give up anything of comparable moral value.

Prohibition of bad consequences

One should not do what has morally bad consequences if by doing so one does not have to give up anything of comparable moral value" (Pfister, 2013, p. 133, emphasis in original).

In addition, the following requirements for an argument can strengthen the rationale for an ethical evaluation:

"*Balancing Act*

Never act in such a way that you could not consent to your course of action if the interests of those affected by it were your own" (Pfister, 2013, p. 135, emphasis in original).

"*Practical syllogism*

1. I would like to bring about y.
2. x is a necessary means to achieve y.
3. I want to do x." (Pfister, 2013, p. 136, emphasis in original; see Fenner, 2020, p. 66f).

"Principle of instrumental rationality

The person who wants the end also wants the means necessary for it" (Pfister, 2013, p. 137, emphasis in original).

In addition, recourse to the following argumentative patterns may help:

"*The end does not justify the means*

If it is forbidden to do y, and y is a necessary means for x, then it cannot be commanded to do x" (Pfister, 2013, p. 138, emphasis in original).

"*Duty towards others*

A has the duty towards B to do x.

Claim against others

B has a claim against A that A does x, at the same time as when A has a duty towards B to do x" (Pfister, 2013, p. 141, emphasis in original).

In addition, the following two lines of reasoning still need to be considered:

- "In deductive arguments, the 1st premise often consists of an *if-then statement* that expresses a logical, definitional, or causal relationship or describes a rule [...]. A very simple example of a causal cause-and-effect relationship would be the statement: 'When it rains, the road is wet'. Similar to syllogisms, logically valid conclusions or false conclusions result, depending on whether in the 2nd premise the *if-part* or *condition-part* ('antecedens') or *then-part* or *consequence-part* ('consequens') is either affirmed or denied. Unlike in syllogistic there are only four possibilities for the second premise, because either the condition part can be affirmed or denied or the consequence part can be affirmed or denied. In our example this would be: it is raining or it is not raining, with respect to the condition part and the road is wet or the road is not wet, with respect to the consequence part. While a yes to the conditions and a no to the consequences in the 2nd premise lead to logically valid arguments, the case of no to the condition and yes to the consequence are fallacies. The reason for the fallacies is that sufficient conditions like rain for wet roads are confused with necessary conditions. This is because rain is only a sufficient but not a necessary condition for wet roads, since they can alternatively become wet, for example, by cleaning the street or watering gardens" (Fenner, 2020, p. 69f, emphasis in original).
- "The *dam-break argument* is used to warn against certain actions or decisions because they allegedly represent the first step in a disastrous series of intermediate steps. Since these inevitably lead to a terrible final state, usually described in drastic terms, the first step alone must be refrained from. Besides the image of a river breaking down dams ('dam-breaking' argument), there is also that of a slippery slope, on which everything inexorably falls down" (Fenner, 2020, p. 72, emphasis in original).

Finally, possible objections to the arguments and reasons that make up the rationale for the ethical decision must be found. This approach was also used in the explanations above under chapter 2 Ethics in the global context for explainingthe "Ten Argumentation Patterns of Exclusion" (see Kirchschlaeger, 2016d, pp. 170-178). Such an approach allows for the preemptive development and unfolding of possible counterarguments, which substantially increases the argumentative persuasiveness of the ethical decision.

Excursus: Ethics Committees, Ethics Boards, Ethics Commissions, Ethics Councils, Ethics Teams, Ethics Groups in the Hands of Ethicists!

At a time and in a context where ethical deliberation appears to be extremely important and necessary due to technological progress, some kind of institutional body dedicated to this specific task must include the necessary ethical expertise and discourse.

Up until now, ethics committees run the risk of failing to meet their objectives. They seem to become either a pawn of particular economic interests (e.g., the establishment and dissolution of Google's Advanced Technology External Advisory Council (ATEAC)) (see Wakefield, 2019), a stakeholder dialogue exercise (e.g., the High-Level Expert Group on Artificial Intelligence (HLEG AI) of the Eruopean Commission (see European Commission, 2020); the Institute of Electrical and Electronics Engineers IEEE working group on a standard for ethics in IT design) or to an interdisciplinary dialogue with a tiny minority of ethicists inside (e.g., Google's ethics board (see Shead, 2019); the UNESCO Ad Hoc Expert Group for the Recommendation on the Ethics of Artificial Intelligence" (see UNESCO, 2020); the Horizon 2020 Commission Expert Group to advise on specific ethical issues raised by driverless mobility (see European Union, 2020)), instead of a panel of ethicists with a small structured interdisciplinary component, which is what would be necessary to fulfill the complex *ethical* task. Of course, a combination of these three manifestations may also occur, e.g., that the second is pursued to serve economic interests in the sense of the first.

In the first case, when ethics committees become the plaything of particular economic interests, there is a danger that ethics committees will no longer serve primarily to provide ethical advice, but will be instrumentalized for reputational gains and corresponding economic advantages. For example, Alphabet's AI company DeepMind has formed an ethics and society team and made it transparent (see DeepMind, n.d.), while Facebook claims to take time specifically for ethics without saying more about it (see Novet, 2018). Most of the fellows on the ethics and society team of Alphabet's AI group DeepMind (4 out of 5) and most of the members of the team are not ethicists (5 out of 6), and research in the area of ethics by prestigious academic institutions is funded globally on ethical issues that go right to the heart of the business interests of the DeepMind AI group (e.g., Oxford Internet Institute at Oxford University; the Center for Information Technology Policy at Princeton University; the AI Now Institute at NYU). The latter provokes at least some questions about academic freedom, independence of research, etc. The same is true for the Institute for Ethics in Artificial Intelligence at the Technical University of Munich (see Institute for Ethics in Artificial Intelligence , n.d.) funded by Facebook (see Buchwald, 2019).

In the second case, which is a stakeholder dialogue exercise, ethics committees are used to achieve the goal of bringing together representatives of a variety of particular interests and collecting their views. This does not serve the purpose of ethical consultation, because ethics is an academic discipline and ethics is not a democracy (see subsection 5.1 above). Or would you entrust the clarification of, for example, a mathematical problem to a stakeholder dialogue? In the High-Level Expert Group on Artificial Intelligence" (HLEG AI) of the European Commission, for example, 48 of 52 members are not ethicists; the group consists of representatives from politics, universities, civil society, and, most importantly, industry (see European Commission, 2020). One of its members stated that this composition has a significant negative impact on their work and results (the 2019 "Ethics Guidelines for Trustworthy Artificial Intelligence" (see European Commission, 2019). "The guidelines are lukewarm, short-sighted, and intentionally vague. They gloss over difficult problems ('explainability') with rhetoric, violate elementary principles of rationality, and they pretend to know things that in reality simply no one knows. The use of lethal autonomous weapons systems was an obvious item on our list (for 'red lines' – i.e., non-negotiable ethical principles that define what must not be done with AI in Europe), also the AI-based assessment of citizens by the state (social scoring) and basically the use of AI that humans can no longer understand and control. I only understood that all this was not really desired when the friendly Finnish HLEG president Pekka Ala-Pietilae (formerly Nokia) asked me in a gentle voice if we could remove the phrase 'non-negotiable' from the document? The next step was for many industry representatives and group members interested in a 'positive vision' to vehemently insist on deleting the word 'red lines' from the entire text – even though these red lines were exactly what we were working on. If you look at the document after today's release, you will find no more red lines. Three have been completely deleted, the rest have been watered down, and instead there is only talk of 'critical concerns'" (Metzinger, 2019).

In the third case, an interdisciplinary dialogue with a tiny minority of ethicists instead of – what would be necessary to fulfill the complex ethical task – a panel of ethicists with a small, structured, interdisciplinary component, or a panel of ethicists working in an interdisciplinary way with a separate interdisciplinary panel, the question arises why one would entrust a scientific task, namely to identify ethical opportunities and risks and to develop ethical solutions, mostly to persons without specific academic training and qualification in this specific field. Or would you entrust the clarification of, say, a mathematical problem to a political scientist? Would we entrust the management of an astrophysical challenge to a legal expert? Or would we invite a diplomat to deal with a biological research question? For example, the UNESCO Ad Hoc Expert Group for the Recommendation on the Ethics of Artificial Intelligence (see UNESCO, 2020) consists of 24 members, only four of whom are ethicists. Their task is to develop the first draft of the first global standardization instrument for the ethics of so called "artificial intelligence" following a decision by the UNESCO General Conference at its 40th session in November 2019. Of course, in such an endeavor of applied ethics, an interdisciplinary component must somehow be part of the activities of the commission charged with this task. But why should this group be composed in such a way that the ethicists are in the minority when the task specifically concerns ethics as a scientific discipline? Why not include the necessary ethical expertise and the relevant professional discourse?

This concept, organization, and practice of ethics committees and ethics councils needs to change as soon as possible, because there is a danger of "ethics white-washing": that is, industry organizing and cultivating ethics debates to buy time – to distract the public, to prevent or at least delay effective regulation and real policy decisions. Politicians also like to set up ethics committees themselves because they don't know what they should be doing, or – if they do – because of intense lobbying (in the U.S., "tech giants led by Amazon, Facebook and Google [...] spent nearly half a billion on lobbying in the last decade" (Romm, 2020); "Facebook, Google, Apple, Amazon, and Microsoft together spend more than 20 million euros annually on their lobbying efforts in Europe" (Winter, 2020)) and the opaque influence of multinational tech corporations they run the risk of not wanting to do it (see LobbyControl, 2020). Yet at the same time, industry is building one "ethics washing machine" after another: Facebook has invested in the Technical University of Munich – in an institute that is supposed to train AI ethicists. "Google had hired the philosophers Joanna Bryson and Luciano Floridi for an 'Ethics Panel' – which was surprisingly discontinued at the end of last week. If that would not have happened, Google, through Floridi – who is also a member of the HLEG AI – would have had direct access to the process by which the group is drafting policy and investment recommendations for the European Union starting this month. That would have been a strategic triumph for the American conglomerate. Because industry is much faster and more efficient than politics or science, there is a risk that, after 'fake news,' we now have a problem with fake ethics, including lots of smokescreens, highly paid industry philosophers, self-invented seals of approval and non-validated certificates for 'Ethical AI made in Europe'" (Metzinger, 2019). Ethics committees and ethics councils must be handed back to the ethicists!

6.4 Act Accordingly!

GUIDING QUESTION:
A. *How can this ethical assessment be concretely addressed and implemented?*

GOAL:
The aim is to show in a concrete and practical way how the ethical position and the ethical evaluation can be addressed effectively and how an ethical solution can be implemented.

The fourth step "Act Accordingly" counts as ethical decision even if the following co-defines ethics. "Ethics does not give any concrete instructions for action or regulations at all; rather, it wants to call upon the person who wants to act well to point out problems with the norms that are relevant in different situations for each case and to decide for oneself what is the right thing to do in a particular case. Freedom is only real in the self-thinking, wanting and acting of each individual and ethics a philosophical doctrinal guide of freedom" (Pieper, 2017, p. 157).

At the same time, the action- and practice-orientation of ethics as a theoretical science is undisputed – taking into account the *two principles of all principles of ethics: freedom and human dignity.* "However, if one considers that ethics is interested in making freedom visible as the unconditional in human action and asserting it as the absolutely binding criterion for all practice without exception against all dogmatic and ideological attempts at fixation on the part of those who are interested in people's lack of freedom for reasons of power, then its concern is at the same time highly demanding, since it is concerned precisely with communicating the insight that no theory and no science – no matter how highly qualified they may be ethically – can deprive humans of the freedom" to which they are called: to understand themselves as a free person among other free persons and to realize this freedom through action" (Pieper, 2017, p. 158).

The action or ethical solution corresponding to the ethical decision should be coherent with the ethical decision and its justification (see Garz & Oser, 1999, p. 16). The main focus of "Act Accordingly" is on the concrete and practical realization of an ethical solution. However, this should be according to the ethical reference points (e.g., principle of responsibility, principle of justice, and human rights principles), which provide the ethical decision-making process with an ethical basis and orientation. Any necessary contextualization in the course of the realization of these ethical principles in concrete contexts must not, however, involve a dilution or undermining of the ethical principles. For example, an ethical solution based on human rights must not discriminate against people. Like the ethical decision in this case, the solution must also be human rights-based.

GUIDING QUESTION:

B. *Ethics beyond rules: How is the rule-transcending uniqueness of the concrete considered?*

GOAL:

The goal is to ensure that the identification of the ethical question/challenge/problem, its ethical evaluation, and the rational and ethical justification of this ethical position as well as the ethical solution do justice to the *rule-transcending uniqueness of the concrete.*

The *rule-transcending uniqueness of the concrete* means that ethical principles, norms, and values can collide or diverge in a concrete encounter with concrete people in a concrete situation and rules can reach their limits because the concrete in its uniqueness can override the rule. Therefore, the ethically right and ethically good in a concrete encounter with concrete people in a concrete situation can include to disrespect an ethical norm, or an ethical value in the service of what is ethically right and ethically good. Ethical principles, norms, and values do not thereby lose their validity, but are affirmed by this striving for the ethically right and ethically good in the concrete encounter with concrete persons in a concrete situation. This ensures that the ethical principles and norms serve people and not vice versa.

Fulfilling this requirement can serve to bring to mind what such collisions and divergences of principles, norms, and values may look like. These can be divided into three main categories:

- "First, it can happen that norms that belong to one and the same moral system collide with each other.
  - for example, when the rule of always being truthful cannot be reconciled in a particular situation with the rule of not inflicting suffering on anyone, so that telling the truth involves inflicting great suffering, but concealing the truth forces one to constantly lie. [...]
- Second, the case may arise that norms that belong to different moral systems collide with each other.
  - For the pacifist the demand not to bear arms and to stay out of acts of war is incompatible with the demand of the state to defend his or her fatherland with arms if necessary. [...]
- Third, a specific, generally accepted norm or value system can affect the self-understanding of an individual so profoundly that its observance would inadmissibly impede his free self-realization, to which he has a moral claim. Here the conflict does not arise from the incompatibility of general norms or systems of norms, but by the clash of a generally accepted norm with an individual norm interpreted in a certain way." (Pieper, 2017, p. 32f)

7 Outlook: Ethics-SAMBA. With Ease and Argumentative Elegance To Take Ethical Decisions in 4 Steps

SAMBA will neither make the ethical issues easier, nor the ethical opportunities and risks smaller. Nor will the necessary ethical decisions become less with SAMBA or make them less challenging. With SAMBA, however, it should be possible to concisely get to the heart of a carefully informed and well-founded ethical decision, to gain clarity about the reasons for an ethical decision and a corresponding action, and to act encouraged and self-confident and put an ethical solution into practice.

Knowing precisely the reasons for an ethical decision also allows out of respect for freedom and human dignity of all people and their autonomy, and thus to the plurality of ethics, to not only communicate the ethical decision as well as the corresponding action, but to also indicate in each case the arguments and reasons, so that these arguments and reasons can then be exchanged and discussed. These arguments and reasons should strive to be "good reasons." "Good reasons" means that it must be conceivable that all people, in their effective freedom and autonomy as well as in their full equality would agree to these reasons – within a model of thought and not within a real worldwide referendum – on ethical grounds (see Kirchschlaeger, 2021a).

Knowing the reasons for one's own ethical decision gives a sense of security. This also enables one to consistently follow the path that has emerged as the ethically correct one, and to follow the ethical decision by implementing them with concrete measures.

Furthermore, SAMBA opens the social horizon that the freedom of all people is lived responsibly by taking and implementing ethical decisions responsibly.

Finally, SAMBA has the effect of "empowering" people to overcome indifference or not even giving it a chance, but to take an ethically justified position and to contribute to a better world through appropriate ethically oriented action – characterized by the principle of responsibility and the principle of intergenerational, omni-dynamic social justice, which entails the principle of sustainability and the principles of human rights.

Bibliography

Achtner, Wolfgang (2010): Willensfreiheit in Theologie und Naturwissenschaften: Ein historisch-systematischer Wegweiser. Darmstadt: Wissenschaftliche Buchgesellschaft.

Alexy, Robert (1998): "Die Institutionalisierung der Menschenrechte im demokratischen Verfassungsstaat". In: Gosepath, Stefan / Lohmann, Georg (eds.): Philosophie der Menschenrechte. Frankfurt am Main: Suhrkamp, 244-264.

Alwang, Jeffrey / Siegel, Paul B. / Jorgenson, Steen L. (2002): "Vulnerability as Viewed from Different Disciplines". In: International Symposium: Sustaining Food Security and Managing Natural Resources in Southeast Asia: Challenges for the 21st Century. January 8–11, Chiang Mai, Thailand. Online: https://studylib.net/doc/18294386/vulnerability-as-viewed-from-different-disciplines [13.07.2023].

Anderson, Michael / Anderson, Susan (2011): "General Introduction". In: Anderson, Michael / Anderson, Susan (eds.): Machine Ethics. Cambridge: Cambridge University Press, 1-4.

Anzenbacher, Arno (1998): Christliche Sozialethik: Einfuehrung und Prinzipien. Paderborn: Ferdinand Schoeningh.

Anzenbacher, Arno (2015): "Moralitaet, Gewissen und der Wille Gottes: Ueberlegungen zu Summa theologiae I-II, q. 19". In: ET-Studies 6(2), 273-300.

Apel, Karl-Otto (1988): Diskurs und Verantwortung: Das Problem des Ueberganges zur postkonventionellen Moral. Frankfurt am Main: Suhrkamp.

Appiah, Kwame Anthony (2007): Der Kosmopolit. Philosophie des Weltbuergertums. Munich: C. H. Beck.

Aristoteles (1983): Nikomachische Ethik. Dirlmeier, Franz (ed.). Stuttgart: Reclam.

Baier, Kurt (1974): Der Standpunkt der Moral: Eine rationale Grundlegung der Ethik. Duesseldorf: Patmos.

Barnes, Michael (2002): Theology and the Dialogue of Religions. Cambridge Studies in Christian Doctrine. Cambridge: Cambridge University Press.

Bauer, Emmanuel J. (ed.) (2007): Freiheit in philosophischer, neurowissenschaftlicher und psychotherapeutischer Perspektive. Munich: Wilhelm Fink.

Bayertz, Kurt (1995): "Eine kurze Geschichte der Herkunft der Verantwortung". In: Bayertz, Kurt: Verantwortung. Prinzip oder Problem? Darmstadt: WBG, 3-71.

Bayertz, Kurt (2010): "Art. Verantwortung". In: Sandkuehler, Hans Joerg (ed.): Enzyklopaedie Philosophie 3 (Q-Z). Hamburg: Felix Meiner, 2861-2862.

Bentham, Jeremy (1975): "Eine Einfuehrung in die Prinzipien der Moral und der Gesetzgebung". In: Hoeffe, Otfried (ed.), Einfuehrung in die utilitaristische Ethik. Munich: UTB. 35-58.

Bentham, Jeremy (2007): An Introduction to the Principles of Morals and Legislation. Dover Philosophical Classics. New York: Dover.

Bhargava, Vikram / Kim, Tae Wan (2017): "Autonomous Vehicles and Moral Uncertainty". In: Lin, Patrick / Jenkins, Ryan / Abney, Keith (eds.): Robot ethics 2.0: From autonomous cars to artificial intelligence. New York: Oxford University Press, 5-19.

Birnbacher, Dieter (2006): "Responsibility for future generations". In: Tremmel, Joerg Chet (ed.): Handbook of Intergenerational Justice. Cheltenham: Edward Elgar Publishing, 23-38.

Bleisch, Barbara / Huppenbauer, Markus / Baumberger, Christoph (2021): Ethische Entscheidungsfindung. Ein Handbuch fuer die Praxis (3. Edition). Zurich: Versus-Verlag.

Bloch, Walter (2011): Willensfreiheit? Neue Argumente in einem alten Streit. Hodos – Wege bildungsbezogener Ethikforschung in Philosophie und Theologie 11. Frankfurt am Main: Peter Lang.

Bobbert, Monika / Scherzinger, Gregor (eds.) (2019): Gute Begutachtung?: Ethische Perspektiven der Evaluation von Ethikkommissionen zur medizinischen Forschung am Menschen. Wiesbaden: Springer.

Bonhoeffer, Dietrich (1992): Ethik. Werke 6. Guetersloh: Guetersloher Verlagshaus.

Bostrom, Nick (2009): "The Future of Humanity". In: Olsen, Jan-Kyrre Berg / Selinger, Evan / Riis, Soren (eds.): New Waves in Philosophy of Technology. New York: Palgrave McMillan, 186-216.

Bostrom, Nick (2014): Superintelligence: Paths, Dangers, Strategies. New York: Oxford University Press.

Bourg, Dominique (2006): "The French Constitutional Charter for the environment: an effective instrument?". In: Tremmel, Joerg Chet (ed.): Handbook of Intergenerational Justice. Cheltenham: Edward Elgar Publishing, 230-243.

Brey, Philip A. E. (2014): "From Moral Agents to Moral Factors: The Structural Ethics Approach". In: Kroes, Peter / Verbeek, Peter-Paul (eds.): The Moral Status of Technical Artefacts. Philosophy of Engineering and Technology 17. Dordrecht: Springer, 124-142.

Brown Weiss, Edith (1989): In Fairness to Future Generations: International Law, Common Patrimony, and Intergenerational Equity. Tokyo: United Nations University / Transnational Publishing.

Brugger, Walter (1992): Stufen der Begruendung von Menschenrechten. In: Der Staat 31, 19–31.

Bryson, Joanna (2010): "Robots Should Be Slaves". In: Wilks, Yorick (ed.): Close Engagements with Artificial Companions: Key Social, Psychological, Ethical and Design Issues. Amsterdam: John Benjamins Publishing, 63-74.

Buchwald, Sabine (2019): "Sind die Forscher am von Facebook finanzierten Ethik-Institut wirklich frei?". In: Sueddeutsche Zeitung, December 13. Online: https://www.sueddeutsche.de/muenchen/muenchen-tu-finanzierung-facebook-1.4723566 [13.07.2023].

Buehl, Walter L. (1998): Verantwortung fuer soziale Systeme: Grundzuege einer globalen Gesellschaftsordnung. Stuttgart: Cotta'sche Buchhandlung.

Butler, Judith (2004): Le pouvoir des mots. Politique du performatif. Paris: Éditions Amsterdam.

Casanova, José (2015): "Der saekulare Staat, religioeser Pluralismus und Liberalismus". In: Schwarz, Gerhard / Sitter-Liver, Beat / Holderegger, Adrian / Tag, Brigitte (eds.): Religion, Liberalitaet und Rechtsstaat: Ein offenes Spannungsverhaeltnis. Zurich: Verlag Neue Zuercher Zeitung, 19-25.

Coeckelbergh, Mark (2012): Growing Moral Relations: Critique of Moral Status Ascription. New York: Palgrave Macmillan.

Corillon, Carol (1989): "The Role of Science and Scientists in Human Rights". In: The Annals of American Academy of Political and Social Science 506(1), 129-140.

Council of Europe (2018): Discrimination, Artificial Intelligence and Algorithmic Decision-Making. Online: https://rm.coe.int/discrimination-artificial-intelligence-and-algorithmic-decision-making/1680925d73 [13.07.2023].

Decker, Michael (2019a): "Autonome Systeme und ethische Reflexion". In: Thimm, Caja / Baechle, Thomas Christian (eds.): Freund oder Feind?. Wiesbaden: Springer, 135-158.

Decker, Michael (2019b): "Ethische Fragen bei autonomen Systemen". In: Mueller, Oliver / Liggieri, Kevin (eds.): Mensch-Maschine-Interaktion. Stuttgart: J.B. Metzler, 309-315.

DeepMind (n.d.): Exploring the real-world impacts of AI. Online: https://deepmind.com/about/ethics-and-society#fellows [13.07.2023].

Demmer, Klaus (2010): Bedraengte Freiheit. Die Lehre von der Mitwirkung – neu bedacht. Studien zur Theologischen Ethik 127. Freiburg im Uechtland: Herder.

Der Große Herder (1935): "Verantwortung". In: Nachschlagewerk fuer Wissen und Leben 12. 4. Edition. Freiburg im Breisgau: Herder, 153-154.

Dierksmeier, Claus (2006): "John Rawls on the rights of future generations". In: Tremmel, Joerg Chet (ed.): Handbook of Intergenerational Justice. Cheltenham: Edward Elgar Publishing, 72-85.

Dignum, Virginia (2019): Responsible Artificial Intelligence: How to Develop and Use AI in a Responsible Way. Cham: Springer.

Duewell, Markus / Huebenthal, Christoph (2011): Handbuch Ethik (M. H. Werner, ed.). Stuttgart: J.B Metzler.

Duewell, Marcus / Neumann, Josef J. (eds.) (2005): Wie viel Ethik vertraegt die Medizin?. Paderborn: Mentis.

Enderle, Georges (2002): "Veraenderungen der Oekonomie im Kontext von Globalisierungsprozessen". In: Virt, Guenter (ed.): Der Globalisierungsprozess: Facetten einer Dynamik aus ethischer und theologischer Perspektive. Freiburg im Breisgau: Herder, 19-40.

European Commission (2019): Ethics Guidelines for Trustworthy Artificial Intelligence. https://digital-strategy.ec.europa.eu/en/library/ethics-guidelines-trustworthy-ai [13.07.2023].

European Commission (2020): Robotics and Artificial Intelligence. https://digital-strategy.ec.europa.eu/en/policies/expert-group-ai [13.07.2023].

European Group on Ethics in Science and New Technologies (2018): Statement on Artificial Intelligence, Robotics and 'Autonomous' Systems. Online: http://ec.europa.eu/research/ege/pdf/ege_ai_statement_2018.pdf [13.07.2023].

European Union (2020): Ethics of Connected and Automated Vehicles: Recommendations of road safety, privacy, fairness, explainability and responsibility.

Fellsches, Josef (2010): "Tugend". In: Sandkuehler, Hans Joerg (ed.), Enzyklopaedie Philosophie. Hamburg: Felix Meiner, 2781-2783.

Fenner, Dagmar (2020): Ethik. Wie soll ich handeln?. Tuebingen: UTB.

Ferrarese, Estelle (2009): „'Gabba-Gabba, We Accept you, One of us': Vulnerability and Power in the Relationship of Recognition". In: Constellations 16(4), 604-614.

Fink, Helmut / Rosenzweig, Rainer (eds.) (2006): Freier Wille – frommer Wunsch? Gehirn und Willensfreiheit. Paderborn: Mentis.

Fleischer, Margot (2012): Menschliche Freiheit – ein vielfaeltiges Phaenomen: Perspektiven von Aristoteles, Augustin, Kant, Fichte, Sartre und Jonas. Freiburg im Breisgau: Karl Alber.

Floridi, Luciano (2014): "Artificial Agents and Their Moral Nature". In: Kroes, Peter / Verbeek, Peter-Paul (eds.): The Moral Status of Technical Artefacts. Philosophy of Engineering and Technology 17. Dordrecht: Springer, 185-212.

Floridi, Luciano / Sanders, Jeff W. (2004): "On the Morality of Artificial Agents". In: Minds and Machines 14(3), 349-379.

Forester-Miller, Holly / David, Thomas. E (1995): A practitioner's guide to ethical decision making. American Counseling Association.

Frezzo, Mark (2015): The Sociology of Human Rights: An Introduction. Cambridge: Polity Press.

Fritzsche, K. Peter (2016): Menschenrechte: Eine Einfuehrung mit Dokumenten. Paderborn: Ferdinand Schoeningh.

Gariup, Deane (2011): "Der harzige Weg zum Frauenstimmrecht". In: POLITHINK.ch, February 7. Online: https://swisspolithink.wordpress.com/2011/02/07/der-harzige-weg-zum-frauenstimmrecht/ [13.07.2023].

Garz, Detlef / Oser, Fritz (1999): Moralisches Urteil und Handeln. Frankfurt am Main: Suhrkamp.

Geert, Berneard (1970): The Moral Rules: A New Rational Foundation for Morality. New York: Harper & Row.

Giers, Joachim (1957): "Zum Begriff der iustitia socialis: Ergebnisse der theologischen Diskussion seit dem Erscheinen der Enzyklika 'Quadragesimo anno' 1931". In: Municher Theologische Zeitschrift 7, 61-74.

Gillmore, Gerald M. / Hunter, John E. (1974): Legalism, Antinomianism, Situationism: Three Moral Decision-Making Orientations. Review of Religious Research National and International Studies 16(1), 3.

Glatzel, Norbert (2000): „'Soziale Gerechtigkeit' – ein umstrittener Begriff". In: Nothelle-Wildfeuer, Ursula / Glatzel, Norbert (eds.): Christliche Sozialethik im Dialog: Zur Zukunftsfaehigkeit von Wirtschaft, Politik und Gesellschaft. Festschrift fuer Lothar Roos zum 65. Geburtstag. Grafschaft: Vektor, 139-150.

Gosepath, Stefan (2010): "Gerechtigkeit". In: Sandkuehler, Hans Joerg (ed.): Enzyklopaedie Philosophie 1. Hamburg: Felix Meiner, 835-839.

Gosseries, Axel (2008): "Theories of intergenerational justice: A synopsis". In: Surveys and Perspectives Integrating Environment and Society 1(1), 61-71.

Gould, Carol C. (2015): "A Social Ontology of Human Rights". In: Cruft, Rowan / Liao, S. Matthew / Renzo, Massimo (eds.): Philosophical Foundations of Human Rights. Oxford: Oxford University Press, 177-195.

Griffin, James (2015): "The Relativity and Ethnocentricity of Human Rights". In: Cruft, Rowan / Liao, S. Matthew / Renzo, Massimo (eds.): Philosophical Foundations of Human Rights. Oxford: Oxford University Press, 555-569.

Grimm, Jacob / Grimm, Wilhelm (1956): "Verantwortung". In: Woerterbuch 12(1). Munich: Deutscher Taschenbuch Verlag, Sp. 79-82.

Guckes, Barbara (2003): Ist Freiheit eine Illusion? Eine metaphysische Untersuchung. Paderborn: Mentis.

Gunkel, David J. (2018): "The Other Question: Can and Should Robots Have Rights?". In: Ethics and Information Technology 20(2), 87-99.

Gut, Walter (2008): "Eine Sternstunde der Menschheit: Die Allgemeine Erklaerung der Menschenrechte von 1948". In: Schweizerische Kirchenzeitung 176(49), 816-819.

Habermas, Juergen (1983): Moralbewusstsein und kommunikatives Handeln. Frankfurt am Main: Suhrkamp.

Habermas, Juergen (1998): "Konzeptionen der Moderne. Ein Rueckblick auf zwei Traditionen". In: Habermas, Juergen: Die postnationale Konstellation: Politische Essays. Frankfurt am Main: Suhrkamp, 195-231.

Habermas, Juergen (1999a): "Richtigkeit versus Wahrheit". In: Habermas, Juergen: Wahrheit und Rechtfertigung. Frankfurt am Main: Suhrkamp, 271-318.

Habermas, Juergen (1999b): "Zur Legitimation durch Menschenrechte". In: Brunkhorst, Hauke / Niesen, Peter (eds.): Das Recht der Republik. Frankfurt am Main: Suhrkamp, 386-403.

Habermas, Juergen (2001): Die Zukunft der menschlichen Natur. Auf dem Weg zu einer liberalen Eugenik? Frankfurt am Main: Suhrkamp.

Habermas, Juergen (2011): ‚The Political'. The Rational Meaning of Questionable Inheritance of Political Theology. In: Mendieta, Eduardo / Van Antwerpen, Jonathan (eds.): The Power of Religion in the Public Sphere. New York: Columbia University Press, 15-33.

Hastedt, H. (ed.) (1994): Ethik. Ein Grundkurs. Reinbek bei Hamburg: Rohwohlt.

Heidbrink, Ludger (2003): Kritik der Verantwortung: Zu den Grenzen verantwortlichen Handelns in komplexen Kontexten. Weilerswist: Velbrueck.

Heller Levitt, D. / Hartwig Moorhead, H. J. (2013): Values and Ethics in counseling. Reallife ethical decision making. New York: Routledge.

Henning, T. (2019): Allgemeine Ethik. Paderborn: UTB.

Herrmann-Sinar, S. (2010): "Prinzip". In: Sandkuehler, Hans Joerg (ed.), Enzyklopaedie Philosophie. Hamburg: Felix Meiner, 2143-2144.

Hersch, Jeanne (1992): Im Schnittpunkt der Zeit. Zurich: Benzinger.

Hieronymi, Andreas (2016): "Das VUCA-Konzept – Vier Denkkategorien fuer Fuehrung und Kommunikation in einer Welt des Wandels". In: Fandel-Meyer, Tanja / Meier, Christoph (eds.): scil Arbeitsbericht 25 – Fuehrungskraefteentwicklung mit Zukunft, 6-21.

Hoeffe, Otfried (1990): Kategorische Rechtsprinzipien. Frankfurt am Main: Suhrkamp.

Hoeffe, Otfried (1991): "Transzendentale Interessen: Zur Anthropologie der Menschenrechte". In: Kerber, Walter (ed.): Menschenrechte und kulturelle Identitaet. Munich: Kindt, 15-36.

Hoefling, Wolfram (2014): "Gewissens- und religionsfreiheitlich fundierte Profilierung kirchlicher Gesundheitseinrichtungen?". In: Bormann, Franz-Josef / Wetzstein, Verena (eds.): Gewissen: Dimensionen eines Grundbegriffs medizinischer Ethik. Berlin: De Gruyter, 89-99.

Hoernle, Tatjana (2011): "Zur Konkretisierung des Begriffs 'Menschenwuerde'". In: Joerden, Jan C. / Hilgendorf, Eric / Petrillo, Natalia / Thiele, Felix (eds.): Menschenwuerde und moderne Medizintechnik. Baden-Baden: Nomos Verlagsgesellschaft, 57-76.

Hoffmaster, Barry (2006): "What Does Vulnerability Mean?" In: Hastings Center Report 36(2), 38-45.

Hogan, Linda (2004): "Conscience in the Documents of Vatican 2". In: Curran, Charles E. (ed.): Conscience. Readings in Moral Theology 14. New York: Paulist Press, 82-88.

Holderegger, Adrian (2006): "Verantwortung". In: Wils, Jean-Pierre / Huebenthal, Christoph (eds.): Lexikon der Ethik. Paderborn: Ferdinand Schoeningh, 394-403.

Holderegger, Adrian / Sitter-Liver, Beat / Hess, Christian W. / Rager, Guenther (eds.) (2007): Hirnforschung und Menschenbild: Beitraege zur interdisziplinaeren Verstaendigung. Basel: Schwabe / Academic Press Fribourg.

Holzhey, Helmut (1975): "Soll man sich des Gewissens wegen ein Gewissen machen? (Vorwort)". In: Holzhey, Helmut (ed.): Gewissen?. Philosophie aktuell 4. Basel: Schwabe, 7-10.

Honecker, Martin (1990): Einfuehrung in die Theologische Ethik: Grundlagen und Grundbegriffe. Berlin: De Gruyter.

Honnefelder, Ludger (1982): "Praktische Vernunft und Gewissen". In: Hertz, Anselm / Korff, Wilhelm / Rendtorff, Trutz / Ringeling, Hermann (eds.): Handbuch der Christlichen Ethik 3. Freiburg im Breisgau: Herder, 19-43.

Honnefelder, Ludger (2012): "Theologische und metaphysische Menschenrechtsbegruendungen". In: Pollmann, Arnd / Lohmann, Georg (eds.): Menschenrechte. Ein interdisziplinaeres Handbuch. Stuttgart: J.B. Metzler, 171-178.

Honnefelder, Ludger (1993): "Vernunft und Gewissen: Gibt es eine philosophische Begruendung fuer die Normativitaet des Gewissens?". In: Hoever, Gerhard / Honnefelder, Ludger (eds.): Der Streit um das Gewissen. Paderborn: Schoeningh, 113-121.

Hoppe, Thomas (2002): "Soziale Gerechtigkeit – ein zentrales Anliegen der katholischen Soziallehre". In: Rauscher, Anton (ed.): Soziale Gerechtigkeit. Koeln: J.P. Bachem, 31-56.

Hubig, Christoph (2011): "Technikethik". In: Stoecker, Ralf / Neuhaeuser, Christian / Raters, Marie-Luise (eds.): Handbuch Angewandte Ethik. Stuttgart: J. B. Metzler, 170-175.

Huebsch, Stefan (1995): Philosophie des Gewissens: Beitraege zur Rehabilitierung des philosophischen Gewissensbegriffs. Neue Studien zur Philosophie 10. Goettingen: Vandenhoeck and Ruprecht.

Huriet, Claude (2009): "Ethics Committees". In: Have, Henk A. M. J. ten / Jean, Michele S. (eds.): The UNESCO Universal Declaration on Bioethics and Human Rights: Background, principles and application. Ethics Series. Paris: UNESCO Publishing, 265-270.

Institute for Ethics in Artificial Intelligence (n.d.): Homepage. Online: https://ieai.mcts.tum.de/ [13.07.2023].

Joas, Hans (2011): Die Sakralitaet der Person: Eine neue Genealogie der Menschenrechte. Berlin: Suhrkamp.

Joas, Hans (2015): Sind die Menschenrechte westlich?. Munich: Koesel-Verlag, 71-80.

Johnson, Deborah (2006): "Computer Systems: Moral Entities but not Moral Agents". In: Ethics and Information Technology 8(4), 195-204.

Johnson, Deborah / Noorman, Merel (2014): "Artefactual Agency and Artefactual Moral Agency". In: Kroes, Peter / Verbeek, Peter-Paul (eds.): The Moral Status of Technical Artefacts. Philosophy of Engineering and Technology 17. Dordrecht: Springer, 143-158.

Jonas, Hans (1985): Das Prinzip Verantwortung: Versuch einer Ethik fuer die technologische Zivilisation. 4. Edition. Frankfurt am Main: Insel.

Jones, Charles (1999): Global Justice: Defending Cosmopolitanism. Oxford: Oxford University Press.

Kant, Immanuel (1974): Grundlegung zur Metaphysik der Sitten. Weischedel, Wilhelm (ed.). Werkausgabe 7. Frankfurt am Main: Suhrkamp.

Kant, Immanuel (1990): Eine Vorlesung ueber Ethik. Gerhardt, Gerd (ed.). Frankfurt am Main: Frankfurter Fischer Taschenbuch Verlag.

Kant, Immanuel (1995a): Kritik der reinen Vernunft 2. Weischedel, Wilhelm (ed.). Werkausgabe 4. Frankfurt am Main: Suhrkamp.

Kant, Immanuel (1995b): "Ueber Paedagogik". In: Kant, Immanuel: Schriften zur Anthropologie, Geschichtsphilosophie, Politik und Paedagogik 2. Weischedel, Wilhelm (ed.). Werkausgabe 12. Frankfurt am Main: Suhrkamp, 691-761.

Kant, Immanuel (1997): Die Metaphysik der Sitten. Weischedel, Wilhelm (ed.). Werkausgabe 8. Frankfurt am Main: Suhrkamp.

Keenan, James F. (2010): A History of Catholic Moral Theology in the Twentieth Century: From Confessing Sins to Liberating Conscience. New York: Continuum.

Kirchschlaeger, Peter G. (2007): "Brauchen die Menschenrechte eine (moralische) Begruendung?". In: Kirchschlaeger, Peter G. / Kirchschlaeger, Thomas / Belliger, Andrea / Krieger, David (eds.): Human Rights and Children. International Human Rights Forum Lucerne (IHRF) 4. Berne: Staempfli, 55-64.

Kirchschlaeger, Peter G. (2011): "Das ethische Charakteristikum der Universalisierung im Zusammenhang des Universalitaetsanspruchs der Menschenrechte". In: Ast, Stephan / Mathis, Klaus / Haenni, Julia / Zabel, Benno (eds.): Gleichheit und Universalitaet. Archiv fuer Rechts- und Sozialphilosophie 128. Stuttgart: Franz Steiner, 301-312.

Kirchschlaeger, Peter G. (2013a): "Die Multidimensionalitaet der Menschenrechte – Chance oder Gefahr fuer den universellen Menschenrechtsschutz?". In: MenschenRechtsMagazin 18(2), 77-95.

Kirchschlaeger, Peter G. (2013b): "Gerechtigkeit und ihre christlich-sozialethische Relevanz". In: Zeitschrift fuer katholische Theologie 135(4), 433–456.

Kirchschlaeger, Peter G. (2013c): "Menschenrechte und Politik". In: Yousefi, Hamid Reza (ed.): Menschenrechte im Weltkontext: Geschichten – Erscheinungsformen – Neuere Entwicklungen. Heidelberg: Springer, 255-260.

Kirchschlaeger, Peter G. (2013d): Wie koennen Menschenrechte begruendet werden? Ein fuer religioese und saekulare Menschenrechtskonzeptionen anschlussfaehiger Ansatz. ReligionsRecht im Dialog 15. Muenster: LIT-Verlag.

Kirchschlaeger, Peter G. (2013e): "Human Rights as an Ethical Basis for Science". In: Journal of Law, Information and Science 22(2), 1-17.

Kirchschlaeger, Peter G. (2014a): "Human Rights and Corresponding Duties and Duty Bearers". In: International Journal of Human Rights and Constitutional Studies 2(4), 309-321.

Kirchschlaeger, Peter G. (2014b): "The Relation between Democracy and Human Rights". In: Grinin, Leonid E. / Ilyin, Ilya V. / Korotayev, Andrey V. (eds.): Globalistics and Globalization Studies: Aspects & Dimensions of Global Views, Yearbook. Volgograd: Uchitel Publishing House, 112-125.

Kirchschlaeger, Peter G. (2014c): "Verantwortung aus christlich-sozialethischer Perspektive". In: ETHICA 22(1), 29-54.

Kirchschlaeger, Peter G. (2015a): “Adaptation – A Model for Bringing Human Rights and Religions Together”. In: Acta Academica 47(2), 163-191.

Kirchschlaeger, Peter G. (2015b): “Das Prinzip der Verletzbarkeit als Begruendungsweg der Menschenrechte”. In: Freiburger Zeitschrift fuer Philosophie und Theologie 62(1), 121-141.

Kirchschlaeger, Peter G. (2016a): “Building Bridges to Religions by Justifying Human Rights. The ‘Clash of Reasons’ and Its Conceptual Impact on Human Rights Discourse”. In: Zajda, Joseph / Ozdowski, Sev (eds.): Globalisation. Human Rights Education and Reforms, 169-186.

Kirchschlaeger, Peter G. (2016b): “How Can We Justify Human Rights?”. In: International Journal of Human Rights and Constitutional Studies 4(4), 313-329.

Kirchschlaeger, Peter G. (2016c): “KonsumActors – mehr Macht beim Einkauf als an der Urne? Konsumethische Ueberlegungen zur Verantwortung beim Einkaufen”. In: ETHICA 24(2), 133-157.

Kirchschlaeger, Peter G. (2016d): Menschenrechte und Religionen. Nichtstaatliche Akteure und ihr Verhaeltnis zu den Menschenrechten. Gesellschaft – Ethik – Religion 7. Paderborn: Ferdinand Schoeningh.

Kirchschlaeger, Peter G. (2016e): “The Interplay of the Legal and the Moral Dimension of Human Rights for the Implementation of Human Rights”. In: International Journal of Human Rights and Constitutional Studies 4(1), 31-44.

Kirchschlaeger, Peter G. (2016f): “To What Extent Should the State Protect Human Beings from Themselves? An Analysis from a Human Rights Perspective”. In: Mathis, Klaus / Tor, Avishalom (eds.): ‘Nudging’ – Possibilities, Limitations and Applications in European Law and Economics. Cham: Springer, 59-67.

Kirchschlaeger, Peter G. (2017a): “Gewissen aus moraltheologischer Sicht”. In: Zeitschrift fuer katholische Theologie 139(2), 152-177.

Kirchschlaeger, Peter G. (2017b): “Die Rede von ‘moral technologies’: Eine Kritik aus theologisch-ethischer Sicht”. In: feinschwarz.net, March 20. Online: https://www.feinschwarz.net/die-rede-von-moral-technologies/ [13.07.2023].

Kirchschlaeger, Peter G. (2018): “Die Menschenrechte als hermeneutischer Schluessel zu ethischen Grundfragen des 21. Jahrhunderts: Begruendung und Ausblick”. In: Zeitschrift fuer katholische Theologie 140, 361-379.

Kirchschlaeger, Peter G. (2019): “Digital Transformation of Society and Economy Ethical Considerations from a Human Rights Perspective”. In: International Journal of Human Rights and Constitutional Studies 6(4), 301-321.

Kirchschlaeger, Peter G. (2020a): “Human Dignity and Human Rights: Fostering and Protecting Pluralism and Particularity”. In: Interdisciplinary Journal for Religion and Transformation in Contemporary Society 6(1), 90-106.

Kirchschlaeger, Peter G. (2020b): “Kollektive versus individuelle Religionsfreiheit – was ist gerecht?”. In: Freiburger Zeitschrift fuer Philosophie und Theologie 67(1), 52-66.

Kirchschlaeger, Peter G. (2021a): Digital Transformation and Ethics. Ethical Considerations on the Robotization and Automation of Society and the Economy and the Use of Artificial Intelligence. Baden-Baden: Nomos.

Kirchschlaeger, Peter G. (2021b): “Ethics of Blockchain Technology”. In: Ulshoefer, Gotlind / Kirchschlaeger, Peter G. / Huppenbauer, Markus (eds.): Digitalisierung aus theologischer und ethischer Perspektive. Konzeptionen – Anfragen – Impulse. Zurich: Pano, 185-209.

Kirchschlaeger, Peter G. (2022a): “Menschenrechte als ethischer Referenzpunkt Theologischer Ethik, Philosophischer Ethik und positiven Rechts”. In: Jahrbuch fuer Recht und Ethik / Annual Review of Law and Ethics, 30(1), 41–70.

Kirchschlaeger, Peter G. (2022b): “Music and a ‚Universal Culture of Human Rights‘”. In Fifer, Julian / Impey, Angela / Kirchschlaeger, Peter G. / Nowak, Manfred / Ulrich, Georg (eds.), The Routledge Companion to Music and Human Rights. London: Routledge, 447-459.

Kirchschlaeger, Peter G. (2023): "Das Menschenbild der Menschenrechte". In: Zichy, Michael (ed.): Handbuch Menschenbilder. Wiesbaden: Springer VS. https://doi.org/https://doi.org/10.1007/978-3-658-32138-3.

Kirchschlaeger, Peter G. / Kirchschlaeger, Thomas (eds.) (2010): Human Rights and Pervasive Computing. International Human Rights Forum (IHRF) 7. Berne: Staempfli.

Klein, Eckart (1997): Menschenrechte: Stille Revolution des Voelkerrechts und Auswirkungen auf die innerstaatliche Rechtsanwendung. Baden-Baden: Nomos Verlagsgesellschaft.

Kohlberg, Lawrence (1981): Essays on Moral Development, Vol. I: The Philosophy of Moral Development, Harper & Row: San Francisco.

Kohlberg, Lawrence (1984): Essays on Moral Development, Vol. II: The Psychology of Moral Development, Harper & Row: San Francisco.

Koller, Peter (1990): "Die Begruendung von Rechten". In: Koller, Peter / Varga, Csaba / Weinberger, Ota (eds.): Theoretische Grundlagen der Rechtspolitik. Ungarisch-Oesterreichisches Symposium der internationalen Vereinigung fuer Rechts- und Sozialphilosophie. Archiv fuer Rechts- und Sozialphilosophie 54. Stuttgart: Franz Steiner, 74-84.

Koller, Peter (2005): Zum Verhaeltnis von Domestischer und Globaler (Un)Gerechtigkeit. Lecture at the Conference 'The Diversitiy of Human Rights: Constitution and Human Rights'. Dubrovnik: Inter University Centre, 3-10 September (manuscript kindly provided by the author).

Kolster, Wedig (2006): Zur Kritik ethischer Urteilsbildung. Emotionen – Bewertung – Handlungsorientierung. Freiburg im Breisgau: Karl Alber.

Korff, Wilhelm (1989): "Zur naturrechtlichen Grundlegung der katholischen Soziallehre". In: Baadte, Guenter / Rauscher, Anton (eds.): Christliche Gesellschaftslehre: Eine Ortsbestimmung. Graz: Styria, 11-52.

Korff, Wilhelm / Wilhelms, Guenter (2001): "Verantwortung". In: Lexikon fuer Theologie und Kirche 10, Freiburg im Breisgau: Herder, 597-600.

Kottow, Miguel H. (2004): "Vulnerability: What kind of principle is it?". In: Medicine, Health Care and Philosophy 7(3), 281-287.

Kramer, Rolf (1992): Soziale Gerechtigkeit – Inhalt und Grenzen. Sozialwissenschaftliche Schriften 18. Berlin: Duncker & Humblot.

Kranich-Stroetz, Christiane (2008): Selbstbewusstsein und Gewissen: Zur Rekonstruktion der Individualitaetskonzeption bei Peter Abaelard. Subjekt – Zeit – Geschichte 2. Muenster: LIT-Verlag.

LaBossiere, Michael (2017): "Testing the Moral Status of Artificial Beings; Or 'I'm Going to Ask You Some Questions…'". In: Lin, Patrick / Abney, Keith / Jenkins, Ryans (eds.): Robot Ethics 2.0: From Autonomous Cars to Artificial Intelligence. New York: Oxford University Press, 293-306.

Ladwig, Bernd (2007): "Das Recht auf Leben – nicht nur fuer Personen". In: Deutsche Zeitschrift fuer Philosophie 55(1), 17-39.

Langan, John (1982): "Human Rights in Roman Catholicism". In: Swidler, Arlene (ed.): Human Rights in Religious Traditions. New York: The Pilgrim Press, 25-39.

Locke, John (2006): Versuch ueber den menschlichen Verstand. Hamburg: Felix Meiner.

Lohmann, Georg (1998): "Menschenrechte zwischen Moral und Recht". In: Gosepath, Stefan / Lohmann, Georg (eds.), Philosophie der Menschenrechte. Frankfurt am Main: Suhrkamp, 62-95.

Lohmann, Georg (2000): "Die unterschiedlichen Menschenrechte". In: Fritzsche, K. Peter / Lohmann, Georg (eds.): Menschenrechte zwischen Anspruch und Wirklichkeit. Wuerzburg: Ergon, 9-23.

Lohmann, Georg (2004): "Menschenrechte in Theorie und Praxis". In: Kirchschlaeger, Peter G. / Kirchschlaeger, Thomas / Belliger, Andrea / Krieger, David (eds.): Human Rights and Terrorism. International Human Rights Forum Lucerne (IHRF) 1. Berne: Staempfli, 305-309.

Lohmann, Georg (2008): "Zu einer relativen Begruendung der Universalisierung der Menschenrechte". In: Nooke, Guenter / Lohmann, Georg / Wahlers, Gerhard (eds.): Gelten Menschenrechte universal? Begruendungen und Infragestellungen. Freiburg im Breisgau: Herder, 218-228.

Margalit, Avishai (1998): The Decent Society. Cambridge: Harvard University Press.

Maritain, Jacques (1948): "Introduction". In: UNESCO (ed.): Human Rights: Comments and interpretations. UNESCO/PHS/3 (rev.). Paris: UNESCO, I-IX.

Markovits, Julia (2014): Moral Reason. Oxford: Oxford University Press.

Marschuetz, Gerhard (2014): Theologisch und ethisch nachdenken (Bd. 1). Wuerzburg: Echter.

Marten, Rainer (1975): "Versuch ueber die philosophische Bestimmung des Gewissens". In: Holzhey, Helmut (ed.): Gewissen? Philosophie aktuell 4. Basel: Schwabe, 119-133.

Martinsen, Renate (2004): Staat und Gewissen im technischen Zeitalter: Prolegomena einer politologischen Aufklaerung. Weilerswist: Velbrueck.

Mathwig, Frank (2000): Technikethik – Ethiktechnik: Was leistet Angewandte Ethik?. Forum Systematik 3. Stuttgart: Wilhelm Kohlhammer.

Metzinger, Thomas (2019): "Nehmt der Industrie die Ethik weg!". In: Tagesspiegel, April 8. Online: https://www.tagesspiegel.de/politik/eu-ethikrichtlinien-fuer-kuenstliche-intelligenz-nehmt-der-industrie-die-ethik-weg/24195388.html [13.07.2023].

Metzler, Marco (2016): "Martin Ford: ‚Automatisierung wird die ganze Arbeitswelt erfassen'„. In: NZZ-Magazin, February 19. Online: https://magazin.nzz.ch/wirtschaft/martin-ford-automatisierung-wird-die-ganze-arbeitswelt-erfassen-ld.145015 [13.07.2023].

Mieth, Dietmar (1992): "Gewissen". In: Wils, Jean-Pierre / Mieth, Dietmar (eds.): Grundbegriffe der christlichen Ethik. Paderborn: Ferdinand Schoeningh, 225-242.

Miller, David (1992): Distributive Justice: What the People Think. In: Ethics 102(April), 555-593.

Misselhorn, Catrin (2018): Grundfragen der Maschinenethik. Stuttgart: Reclam.

Moor, James H. (2006): "The Nature, Importance, and Difficulty of Machine Ethics". In: IEEE Intelligent Systems 21(4), 18-21.

Moyn, Samuel (2010): The Last Utopia: Human Rights in History. Cambridge: Harvard University Press.

Neue Zuercher Zeitung (2011): "Der lange Weg zum Frauenstimmrecht". In: Neue Zuercher Zeitung, February 4. Online: https://www.nzz.ch/frauenstimmrecht-1.9350588?reduced=true [13.07.2023].

Neuhaeuser, Christian (2012): "Kuenstliche Intelligenz und ihr moralischer Standpunkt". In: Beck, Susanne (ed.): Jenseits von Mensch und Maschine: Ethische und rechtliche Fragen zum Umgang mit Robotern, Kuenstlicher Intelligenz und Cyborgs. Robotik und Recht 1. Baden-Baden: Nomos Verlagsgesellschaft, 23-42.

Neuman, Gerald (2003): "Human Rights and Constitutional Rights". In: Stanford Law Review 55(5), 1863-1900.

Nickel, James W. (2015): "Personal Deserts and Human Rights". In: Cruft, Rowan / Liao, S. Matthew / Renzo, Massimo (eds.): Philosophical Foundations of Human Rights. Oxford: Oxford University Press, 153-165.

Nida-Ruemelin, Julian (2005a): Angewandte Ethik. Die Bereichsethiken und ihre theoretische Fundierung. Alfred Kroener.

Nida-Ruemelin, Julian (2005b): Ueber menschliche Freiheit. Stuttgart: Reclam.

Nida-Ruemelin, Julian (2011): Verantwortung. Stuttgart: Reclam.

Noichl, Franz (1993): Gewissen und Ideologie: Zur Moeglichkeit der Rekonstruktion eines unbedingten Sollens. Freiburger theologische Studien 152. Freiburg im Breisgau: Herder.

Nothelle-Wildfeuer, Ursula (1999): Soziale Gerechtigkeit und Zivilgesellschaft. Paderborn: Ferdinand Schoeningh.

Nothelle-Wildfeuer, Ursula (2008): "Die Sozialprinzipien der Katholischen Soziallehre". In: Rauscher, Anton (ed.): Handbuch der Katholischen Soziallehre. Berlin: Duncker & Humblot, 143-163.

Novet, Jordan (2018): "Facebook forms a special ethics team to prevent bias in its A.I. software". In: CNBC, May 3. Online: https://www.cnbc.com/2018/05/03/facebook-ethics-team-prevents-bias-in-ai-software.html [13.07.2023].

Nowak, Manfred (2002): Einfuehrung in das internationale Menschenrechtssystem. Wien: NWV.

Nussbaum, Martha C. (1993): "Menschliches Tun und soziale Gerechtigkeit. Zur Verteidigung des aristotelischen Essentialismus". In: Brumlik, Micha / Brunkhorst, Hauke (eds.): Gemeinschaft und Gerechtigkeit. Frankfurt am Main: Suhrkamp, 324-363.

Nussbaum, Martha C. (1995): "Human Capabilities, Female Human Beings". In: Nussbaum, Martha C. / Glover, Jonathan (eds.): Women, culture, and development: A study of human capabilities. Oxford: Oxford University Press, 61-104.

Ohly, Lukas (2019): Ethik der Robotik und der Kuenstlichen Intelligenz. Theologisch-Philosophische Beitraege zu Gegenwartsfragen 22. Berlin: Peter Lang.

Ong-Van-Cung, Kim Sang (2010): "Reconaissance et vulnérabilité: Honneth et Butler". In: Archives de Philosophie 73(1), 119-141.

Parfit, Derek (1984): Reasons and Persons, Oxford: Clarendon Press.

Pauder-Studer, H. (2020): Einfuehrung in die Ethik. Vienna: UTB.

Perry, Michael J. (2005): "The Morality of Human Rights: A Nonreligious Ground?". In: Emory Law Journal 54, 97-150.

Pfister, Jonas (2013): Werkzeuge des Philosophierens. Stuttgart: Reclam.

Pieper, Annemarie (2017): Einfuehrung in die Ethik. (7. Edition) Tuebingen: UTB.

Platon (1989): Der Staat: Ueber das Gerechte. Apelt, Otto / Bormann, Karl (eds.). Philosophische Bibliothek 80. Hamburg: Felix Meiner.

Pogge, Thomas (1999): "Menschenrechte als moralische Ansprueche an globale Institutionen". In: Gosepath, Stefan / Lohmann, Georg (eds.): Philosophie der Menschenrechte. Frankfurt am Main: Suhrkamp, 378-400.

Pogge, Thomas (2002): World Poverty and Human Rights. Cambridge: John Wiley & Sons Publishing.

Pritchard, Michael S. / Engelhardt, Elaine E. / Archer, Carina / Hartmann, Laura P. / Werhane, Patricia H. (2013): Obstacles to Ethical Decision-Making. Mental Models, Milgram and the Problem of Obedience. Cambridge: Cambridge University Press.

Rabossi, Eduardo (1990): "La teoria de los derechos umanos naturalizada". In: Revista del Centro de Estudio Constitucionales 5(Enero-marzo), 159-175.

Rawls, John (1971): A Theory of Justice. Cambridge: Harvard University Press.

Rawls, John (1993): Political Liberalism. New York: Columbia University Press.

Rawls, John (1999): The Law of Peoples. Cambridge: Harvard University Press.

Raz, Joseph (1986): The Morality of Freedom. Oxford: Clarendon Press.

Raz, Joseph (2015): "Human Rights in the Emerging World Order". In: Cruft, Rowan / Liao, S. Matthew / Renzo, Massimo (eds.): Philosophical Foundations of Human Rights. Oxford: Oxford University Press, 217-231.

Reeder, John P. (2015): "On Grounding Human Rights: Variations on Themes by Little". In: Twiss, Sumner B. / Simion, Marian G. / Petersen, Rodney L. (eds.): Religion and Public Policy: Human Rights, Conflict, and Ethics. New York: Cambridge University Press, 96-119.

Reiter, Johannes (1991): "Die Frage nach dem Gewissen". In: Seidel, Walter (ed.): Befreiende Moral: Handeln aus christlicher Verantwortung. Wuerzburg: Echter, 11-31.

Remele, Kurt (2009): "Gerechtigkeit lehren, gerecht leben: Katholische Sozialethik und Soziallehre als institutionalisierte Gesellschaftsreflexion und praktisches Handeln". In: Salzburger Theologische Zeitschrift 13, 192-205.

Roemelt, Josef (2011): Das Geschenk der Freiheit: Christlicher Glaube und moralische Verantwortung. Innsbruck: Tyrolia.

Romm, Tony (2020): "Tech giants led by Amazon, Facebook and Google spent nearly half a billion on lobbying over the past decade, new data shows". In: The Washington Post, January 22. Online: https://www.washingtonpost.com/technology/2020/01/22/amazon-facebook-google-lobbying-2019/ [13.07.2023].

Rorty, Richard (1996): "Menschenrechte, Rationalitaet und Gefuehl". In: Shute, Stephen / Hurley, Susan (eds.): Die Idee der Menschenrechte. Frankfurt am Main: Suhrkamp, 144-170.

Roth, Gerhard (2003): Aus Sicht des Gehirns. Frankfurt am Main: Suhrkamp.

Ruiz-Cano, Jennifer (2015): "Revision de modelos para el analisis de dilemas eticos (Review of models ofor the analysis of ethical dilemmas)". In: Boletín Medico del Hospital Infantil de Mexico 72/2, 1-10.

Runggaldier, Edmund (2003): "Deutung menschlicher Grunderfahrungen im Hinblick auf unser Selbst". In: Rager, Guenter / Quitterer, Josef / Runggaldier, Edmund (eds.): Unser Selbst – Identitaet im Wandel neuronaler Prozesse. Paderborn: Ferdinand Schoeningh, 143-221.

Sandkuehler, Hans Joerg (2010): "Art. Menschenrechte". In: Sandkuehler, Hans Joerg (ed.): Enzyklopaedie Philosophie, Hamburg: Felix Meiner, 1530–1553.

Sandler, Ronald L. (2014): Ethics and Emerging Technologies. New York: Palgrave Macmillan.

Sartre, Jean-Paul (1943): Das Sein und das Nichts: Versuch einer phaenomenologischen Ontologie. Hamburg: Rowohlt.

Schaupp, Walter (2014): "Zwischen personal beliefs und professional duties: Weltanschaulich-religioeser Pluralismus als neue Herausforderung fuer das aerztliche Gewissen". In: Bormann, Franz-Josef / Wetzstein, Verena (eds.): Gewissen: Dimensionen eines Grundbegriffs medizinischer Ethik. Berlin: De Gruyter, 3-23.

Schloegl-Flierl, Kerstin (2016): "Die Tugend der Epikie im Spannungsfeld von Recht und Ethik". In: Chittilappilly, Paul-Chummar (ed.): Horizonte gegenwaertiger Ethik. Festschrift Josef Schuster. Freiburg im Breisgau: Herder, 29-39.

Schmitt, Hanspeter (2008): Sozialitaet und Gewissen. Anthropologische und theologisch-ethische Sondierung der klassischen Gewissenslehre. Studien der Moraltheologie 40. Wien: LIT-Verlag.

Schockenhoff, Eberhard (2014a): Grundlegung der Ethik: Ein theologischer Entwurf. Freiburg im Breisgau: Herder.

Schoenherr-Mann, Hans-Martin (2010): Die Macht der Verantwortung. Freiburg im Breisgau: Karl Alber.

Schroeder, Doris / Gefenas, Eugenijus (2009): "Vulnerability: Too Vague and Too Broad?". In: Cambridge Quarterly of Healthcare Ethics 18(2), 113-121.

Schueller, Bruno (1980): Die Begruendung sittlicher Urteile. Typen ethischer Argumentation in der katholischen Moraltheologie. Duesseldorf: Patmos-Verlag.

Schuster, Johannes / Kerber, Walter (2016): "Gewissen". In: Brugger, Walter (ed.): Philosophisches Woerterbuch. Freiburg im Breisgrau: Herder, 144-146.

Shead, Sam (2019): "Google Announced an AI Advisory Council, but the Mysterious AI Ethics Board Remains A Secret". In: Forbes, March 27. Online: https://www.forbes.com/sites/samshead/2019/03/27/google-announced-an-ai-council-but-the-mysterious-ai-ethics-board-remains-a-secret/#34ba580e614a [13.07.2023].

Shoham, Shlomo / Lamay, Nira (2006): "Commission for Future Generations in the Knesset: lessons learnt". In: Tremmel, Joerg Chet (ed.): Handbook of Intergenerational Justice. Cheltenham: Edward Elgar Publishing, 244-281.

Singer, Peter (2004): "One Community". In: Singer, Peter: One World: The Ethics of Globalization. New Haven: Yale University Press, 150-193.

Smith, Adam (2004): Theorie der ethischen Gefuehle. Hamburg: Felix Meiner.

Strong, Kelly C. / Meyer, Dale G. (1992): "An Integrative Descriptive Model of Ethical Decision Making". In: Journal of Business Ethics 11(2), 89-94

Sullins, John P. (2006): "When Is a Robot a Moral Agent". In: International Review of Information Ethics 6(12), 23-30.

Taparelli, Luigi (1855): Saggio teoretico di diritto naturale appoggiato sul fatto 1. Roma: La Civiltà cattolica.

Tasioulas, John (2015): "On the Foundations of Human Rights". In: Cruft, Rowan / Liao, S. Matthew / Renzo, Massimo (eds.): Philosophical Foundations of Human Rights. Oxford: Oxford University Press, 45-70.

Teichtweiter, Georg (1976): "Moral – wieder gefragt?". In: Hirschmann, Johannes (ed.): Der Christ in der Welt 5(7a/b). Aschaffenburg: Paul Pattloch, 102-123.

Thimm, Caja / Baechle, Thomas Christian (2018): "Autonomie der Technologie und autonome Systeme als ethische Herausforderung". In: Rath, Matthias / Krotz, Friedrich / Karmasin, Matthias (eds.): Maschinenethik. Wiesbaden: Springer, 73-87.

Thomas Aquinas (1937): Summa Theologica 6. Katholischer Akademikerverband (ed.). Uebersetzt von Dominikanern und Benediktinern Deutschlands und Oesterreichs. Salzburg: Anton Pustet.

Thompson, Janna (2010): "What is Intergenerational Justice?". In: Future Justice, 5-20. Online: http://www.futureleaders.com.au/book_chapters/pdf/Future_Justice/Janna_Thompson.pdf. [13.07.2023].

Torrance, Steve (2008): "Ethics and consciousness in artificial agents". In: AI & Society 22, 495-521.

Torrance, Steve (2011): "Machine Ethics and the Idea of a More-Than-Human-World". In: Anderson, Michael / Anderson, Susan Leigh (eds.): Machine Ethics. Cambridge: Cambridge University Press, 115-137.

Tremmel, Joerg Chet (2006): "Establishing intergenerational justice in national constitutions". In: Tremmel, Joerg Chet (Eds): Handbook of Intergenerational Justice. Cheltenham: Edward Elgar Publishing, 187-214.

Trotter Cockburn, Catherine (1702): A Defence of Mr. Lock's Essay of Human Understanding. London: William Turner & John Nutt.

Tugendhat, Ernst (1993): Vorlesungen ueber Ethik. Frankfurt a. M: Suhrkamp.

Turner, Bryan S. (2006): Vulnerability and Human Rights. Pennsylvania: Pennsylvania State University Press.

Tzafestas, Spyros G. (2016): Roboethics: A Navigating Overview. Intelligent Systems, Control and Automation: Science and Engineering. Cham: Springer.

Ulpian, Domitius (2005): Corpus Iuris Civilis: Digesten 1. Knuetel, Rolf / Kupisch, Berthold / Seiler, Hans Hermann / Behrends, Okko (eds.). Heidelberg: C. F. Mueller.

UNESCO (2020): Elaboration of a Recommendation on the ethics of artificial intelligence. Online: https://en.unesco.org/artificial-intelligence/ethics [13.07.2023].

United Nations (1948): Universal Declaration of Human Rights of 1948. United Nations. Online: https://www.un.org/en/universal-declaration-human-rights/ [13.07.2023].

United Nations (1950): French Delegate to the Sixth Commission on Human Rights 1950. Summary Record of the 165th meeting: Draft International covenant on human rights. Economic and Social Council. Commission on Human Rights. Sixth Session. E/CN.4/SR.165. Paris: United Nations.

Úriz Pemán, Maria J. / Idareta Goldaracena, Francisco (2017): La ética en las intervenciones sociales: Algunos modelos de resolución de dilemas éticos. https://academica-e.unavarra.es/xmlui/handle/2454/33153 [13.07.2023].

Van Opstal, Rocus / Timmerhuis, Jacqueline (2006): "The role of CPB in Dutch economic policy". In: Tremmel, Joerg Chet (eds.): Handbook of Intergenerational Justice. Cheltenham: Edward Elgar Publishing, 299-316.

Veith, Werner (2014): "Gerechtigkeit". In: Heimbach-Steins, Marianne (ed.): Christliche Sozialethik: Ein Lehrbuch 1. Studienliteratur. Regensburg: Friedrich Pustet, 315-326.

Verbeek, Peter-Paul (2014): "Some Misunderstandings About the Moral Significance of Technology". In: Kroes, Peter / Verbeek, Peter-Paul (eds.): The Moral Status of Technical Artefacts. Philosophy of Engineering and Technology 17. Dordrecht: Springer, 75-88.

Virt, Guenter (2007): Damit Menschsein Zukunft hat: Theologische Ethik im Einsatz fuer eine humane Gesellschaft. Marschuetz, Gerhard / Prueller-Jagenteufel, Gunter M. (eds.). Wuerzburg: Echter.

Vogt, Markus (2005): "Natuerliche Ressourcen und intergenerationelle Gerechtigkeit". In: Heimbach-Steins, Marianne (ed.): Christliche Sozialethik: Ein Lehrbuch 2. Studienliteratur. Regensburg: Friedrich Pustet, 137-162.

Wakefield, Jane (2019): "Google's ethics board shut down". In: BBC News, April 5. Online: https://www.bbc.com/news/technology-47825833 [13.07.2023].

Wallach, Wendell / Allen, Collin (2009): Moral Machines: Teaching Robots Right from Wrong. Oxford: Oxford University Press.

Weiss, Norman (2007): "Menschenrechtsschutz". In: Volger, Helmut (ed.): Grundlagen und Strukturen der Vereinten Nationen. Munich: De Gruyter Oldenbourg, 163-188.

Werner, Micha H. (2021): Einfuehrung in die Ethik. Stuttgart: J.B. Metzler.

Weston, Anthony (2017): A 21st Century Ethical Toolbox. New York: Oxford University Press.

Wetz, Franz Josef (1998): Die Wuerde des Menschen ist antastbar: Eine Provokation. Stuttgart: Klett-Cotta.

Willoweit, Dietmar (1992): "Die Veraeusserung der Freiheit. Ueber den Unterschied von Rechtsdenken und Menschenrechtsdenken". In: Bielefeldt, Heiner / Brugger, Winfried / Dicke, Klaus (eds.): Wuerde und Recht des Menschen. Festschrift Johannes Schwartlaender. Wuerzburg: Koenigshausen & Neumann, 255-268.

Winter, Sabrina (2020): "Undurchsichtige Lobbyarbeit der US-Techkonzerne aufgedeckt. Verstoesse gegen EU-Transparenzregeln". In: Der Spiegel, September 28. Online: https://www.spiegel.de/netzwelt/netzpolitik/facebook-google-amazon-apple-microsoft-undurchsichtige-lobbyarbeit-aufgedeckt-a-432bb716-0844-4a1a-95c0-6bfec6e733c5 [13.07.2023].

Witschen, Dieter (2002): Christliche Ethik der Menschenrechte: Systematische Studien. Studien der Moraltheologie 28. Muenster: LIT-Verlag.

Wolbert, Werner (2003): "Menschenwuerde, Menschenrechte und Theologie". In: Salzburger Theologische Zeitschrift 7(2), 161-179.

Wolbert, Werner (2008): Gewissen und Verantwortung: Gesammelte Studien. Studien zur Theologischen Ethik 118. Freiburg im Breisgau: Herder.

Wolf, Clark (2003): "Intergenerational Justice". In: Frey, Raymond G. / Wellman, Christopher Heath (eds.): A Companion to Applied Ethics. Malden: Wiley Blackwell Publishing, 279-294.

Wolf, Jean-Claude (1993): Utilitarismus, Pragmatismus und kollektive Verantwortung. Freiburg im Breisgau: Herder.

Yampolski, Roman V. (2013): "Artificial Intelligence Safety Engineering: Why Machine Ethics Is a Wrong Approach". In: Mueller, Vincent C. (ed.): Philosophy and Theory of Artificial Intelligence. Cham: Springer, 289-296.

Zimmerli, Walther C. (1993): "Wandelt sich Verantwortung mit technischem Wandel?". In: Lenk, Hans / Rophl, Guenther (eds.): Technik und Ethik. Stuttgart: Reclam, 92-111.

Index

The data refer to the page numbers of the book.

A

Ambiguity 7
Artificial Intelligence 117, 118
Attention 17, 59, 114
Authoritative 66
Authority 35, 44, 47, 49, 66, 72, 73, 75–78, 112
Autonomy 11, 16, 23, 25, 28, 32, 39, 45, 46, 48, 50–52, 54, 57, 65, 72, 78, 88–90, 95, 104, 107, 113, 123

C

Complexity 7, 18, 44, 57, 58, 68, 71, 73, 110
Conscience 39, 41, 44–48, 50, 51, 54, 57, 70, 77, 78, 89, 98, 99, 105, 107
Consequences 18, 20, 23, 39, 42, 52, 58, 67, 69–73, 77, 78, 107, 115, 116
Consequentialism 63, 67
Context 7, 8, 12, 17, 20, 25, 26, 28, 29, 31, 32, 40, 42, 44, 45, 58, 59, 64, 73, 77, 79, 82, 83, 91, 92, 98, 104, 109, 112, 116, 117

D

Data-Based Systems 51
Decide 12, 21, 22, 39, 48, 51, 52, 54, 55, 63, 64, 76, 89, 119
Decision 7, 11–20, 22, 23, 25, 27–29, 31, 33–36, 39, 42, 47, 51–55, 57, 59, 60, 62–71, 73, 74, 77–80, 82, 85–87, 89, 95, 99, 100, 104–106, 109–112, 116, 118–120, 123
Decision-making 7, 11–20, 23, 25, 27, 28, 31, 33, 34, 36, 39, 42, 51–55, 57, 59, 60, 62–68, 70, 73, 77–80, 82, 85, 95, 104, 105, 109–113, 120
Democracy 57, 117
Deontology 69
Digital transformation 11
Discourse 25, 27–31, 39, 45, 63, 66, 67, 70, 81, 86, 88, 90, 92, 103, 107, 109, 117, 118
Discourse Ethics 67
Diversity 7, 8, 17, 30, 31, 37, 58, 93, 104, 105, 117, 119
Duty 13, 35, 45–47, 63, 69, 71–73, 82, 90, 91, 106, 107, 112, 113, 116
Duty/Duty Ethics 13, 35, 45–47, 63, 69, 71–73, 82, 90, 91, 106, 107, 112, 113, 116

E

Elegance 7, 18, 23, 59, 123
Enforcement 34–36, 74, 104
Ethical standard 23, 103–105
Ethicist 13
Ethics 7, 8, 11–18, 22, 25, 26, 33–37, 44, 50, 53, 57, 59, 63–71, 78, 82, 83, 96, 105–114, 116–120, 123
Ethics Committees 22, 57, 117, 119
Ethics Council 104, 117
Ethics Group 117
Ethics Panel 117, 118
Ethics Team 117

F

Follow 39, 50, 52, 57, 110, 123
Freedom 7, 11–17, 25–34, 36, 37, 39, 45–50, 54, 57, 63–65, 70, 72, 75, 76, 78, 81, 89–91, 95, 98, 99, 104–107, 113, 117, 119, 120, 123

G

Global 8, 11, 12, 25, 26, 30, 31, 44, 50, 62, 65, 73, 74, 77, 84, 85, 87, 88, 91, 99, 105, 113, 116, 118
Group 8, 12, 28, 29, 50, 53, 68, 71, 75, 85, 95, 113, 117–119

H

Human dignity 11, 15–17, 25–34, 36, 37, 48, 49, 63, 68–70, 81, 83–85, 89, 91, 92, 98, 99, 101, 103–105, 120, 123

Human Rights 25, 26, 28–31, 33–37, 43, 63, 70, 74, 82–84, 86–96, 98–106, 120, 123

J

Justice 7, 17, 30, 34, 40, 46, 58, 62–65, 68, 70, 71, 78–90, 99–104, 111, 120, 123

L

Law 18, 29, 33–37, 40, 57, 66, 77, 81, 82, 84, 94, 110
Legal standard 22, 105
Lightness 23, 111
Luck 63, 68

M

Machine 52, 53, 119
Morale 7, 11–16, 19, 20, 26, 30, 32, 33, 35–37, 39–42, 44–54, 58, 59, 62–67, 69–72, 74, 75, 77–81, 84, 86, 89, 90, 92–96, 98, 100–104, 106–113, 115, 121
Morale capacity 16, 39–41, 44, 53, 55, 84, 95

N

Natural Law 66, 81
Nature 13, 19, 22, 36, 51, 60, 62, 63, 66, 72, 73, 77–79, 86, 90, 92, 100, 105
Normethics 66
Norms 12, 14–16, 20, 21, 25, 31–35, 45, 47, 48, 54, 55, 57, 58, 63–67, 69–71, 74–76, 78, 82–84, 91, 95, 100, 103, 106–109, 111–115, 119–121

P

Plurality 11, 16, 25, 26, 31, 63, 65, 66, 103–106, 112, 123
Principle 11, 14–17, 28, 34, 35, 42–44, 46, 49–51, 53, 57, 62–68, 70, 74, 78, 79, 83, 85, 86, 89, 95–97, 99–102, 104–108, 110, 113, 115, 120, 123
Protection 41, 69, 70, 89, 94, 98–101, 104
Purpose 14, 61, 67, 74, 117

R

Realization 43, 47, 74, 81, 84, 87–91, 94, 97, 106, 120, 121
Respect 11, 15–17, 25, 26, 35, 36, 53, 54, 63, 64, 76, 81, 83, 85, 90–94, 100, 105, 106, 112, 116, 123
Responsibility 11, 12, 16, 18, 39, 45, 49–54, 58, 63, 67, 70–79, 81, 82, 86–89, 91, 120, 123
Rule-transcending uniqueness of the concrete 18, 57, 65, 112, 120

S

Standard 22, 23, 27, 33, 39, 57, 60, 61, 64, 69, 72, 75, 78, 89, 92, 103–107, 109–111, 114, 117, 118

T

Teleology 67

U

Uncertainty 7, 42, 85, 86, 88, 97
Utilitarianism 63, 67, 68

V

Virtue 57, 58, 63, 65, 79, 87
Virtue/Virtue Ethics 57, 58, 63, 65, 79, 87
Volatility 7
Vulnerability 28, 39–44, 50–52, 54, 79, 86, 95–102, 104, 109

Zeitfracht Medien GmbH
Ferdinand-Jühlke-Straße 7
99095 Erfurt, Deutschland
produktsicherheit@kolibri360.de